HOW TO DRAW
Princess & Unicorn
and Mermaid

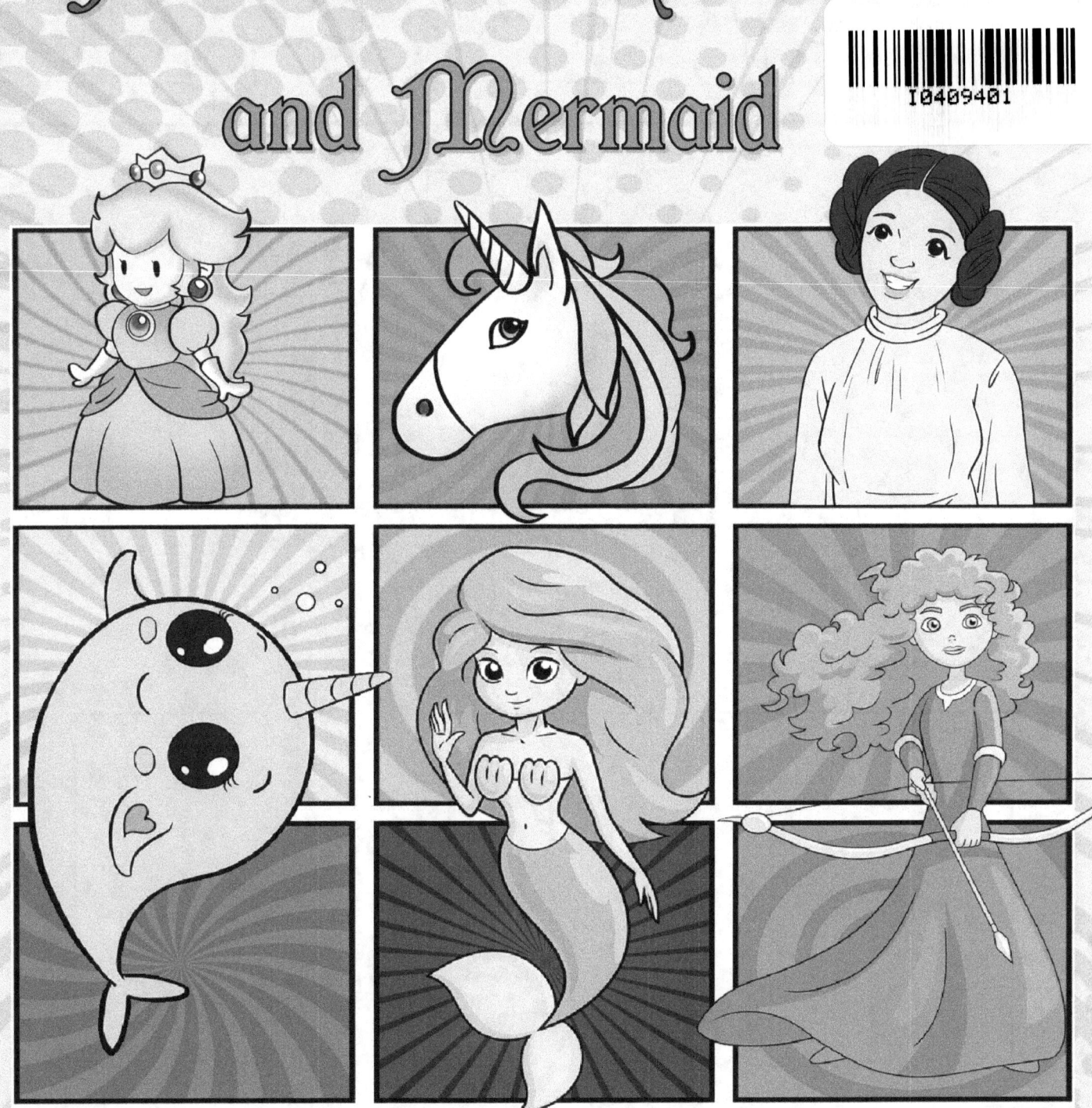

NAKHSA KATSUHITO

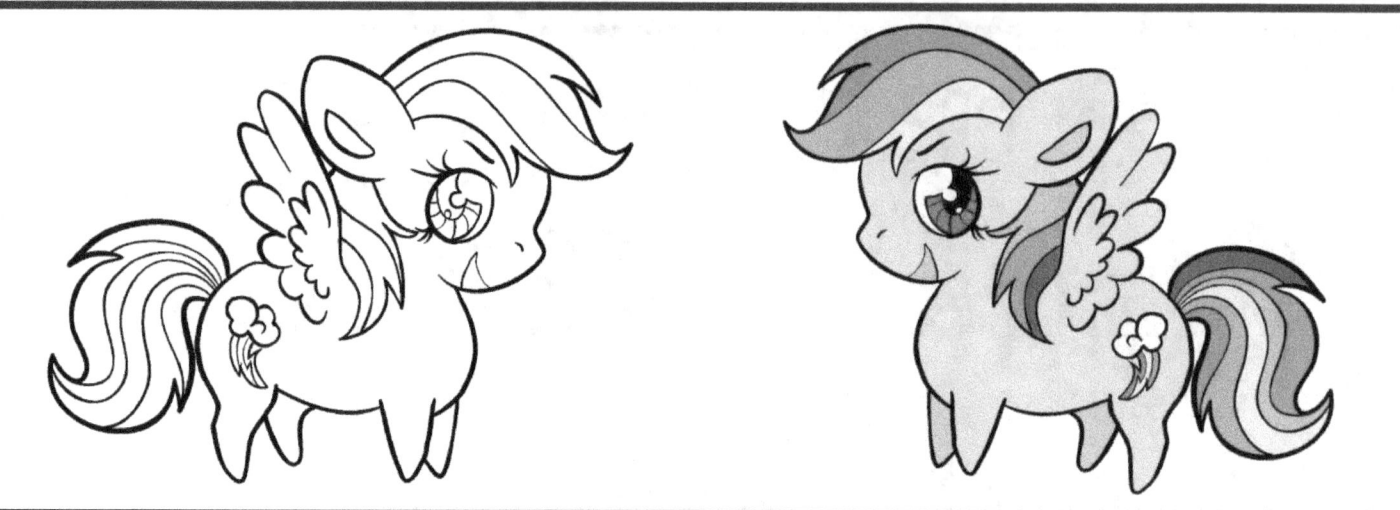

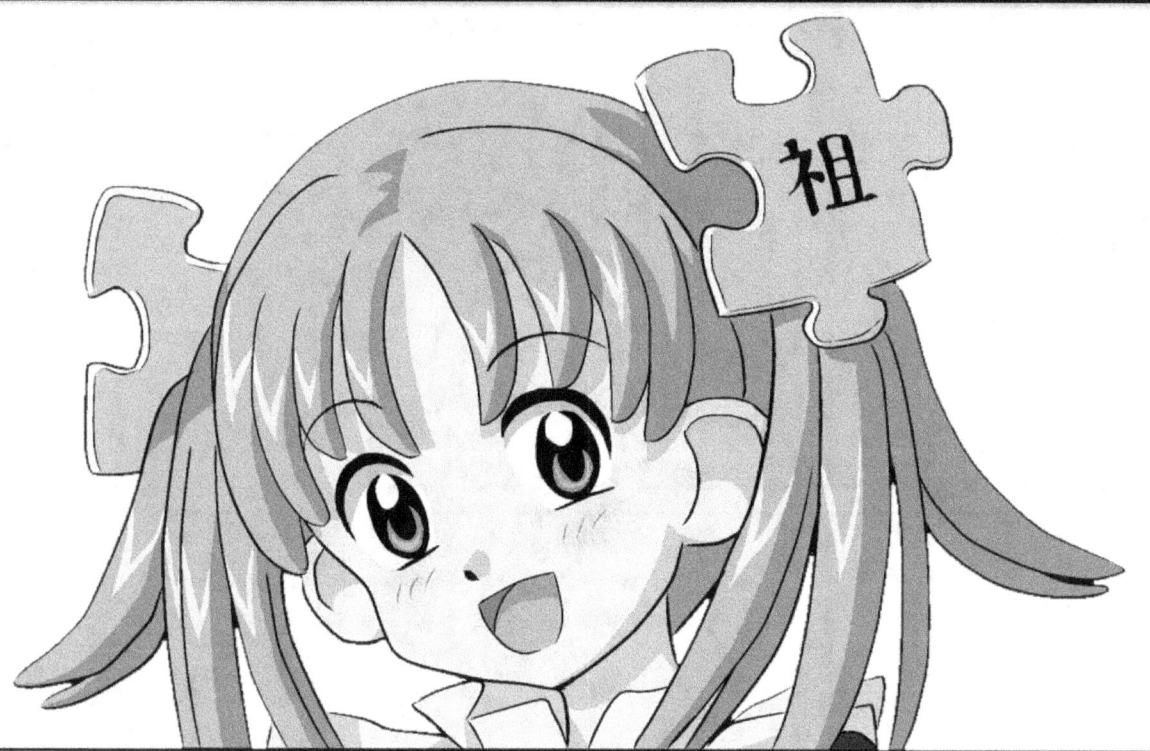

THIS BOOK BELONGS TO:

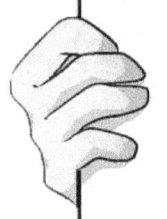

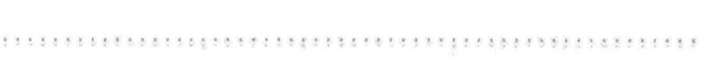

Princess & Unicorn and Mermaid

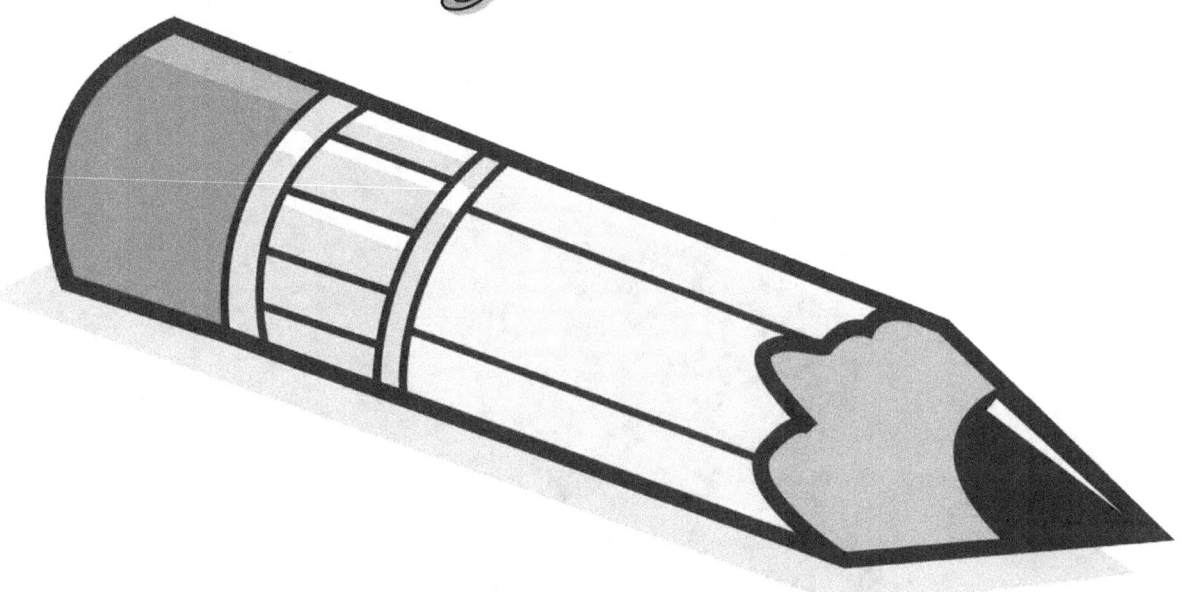

NAKHSA KATSUHITO

EVERYTHING YOU NEED: DRAWING PAPER, PENCILS, ERASERS, PENCIL SHARPENERS, PENS, CRAYONS. AND LOTS OF YOUR CREATIVITY

PART 1 how to draw princesses

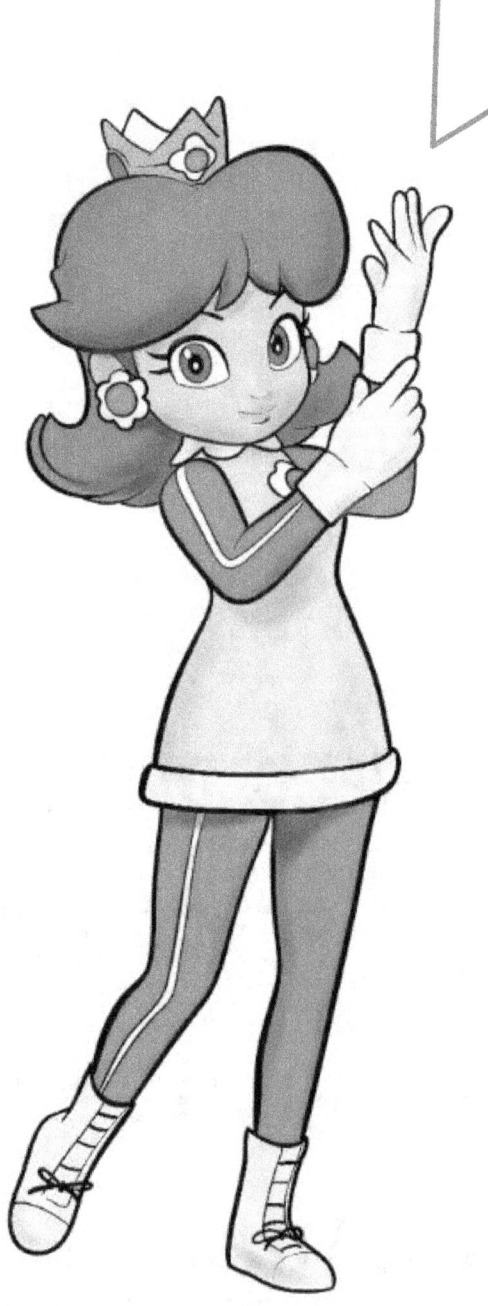

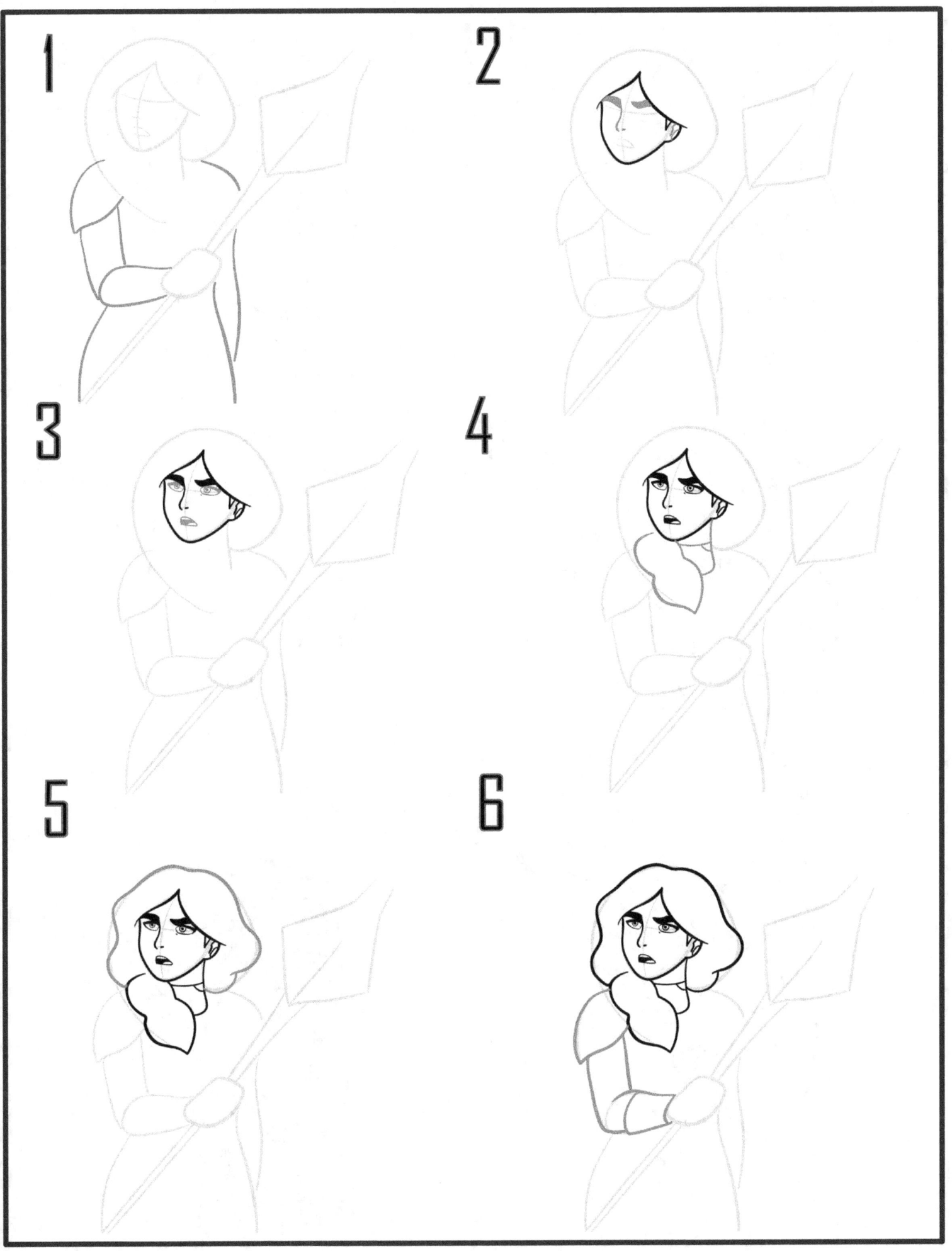

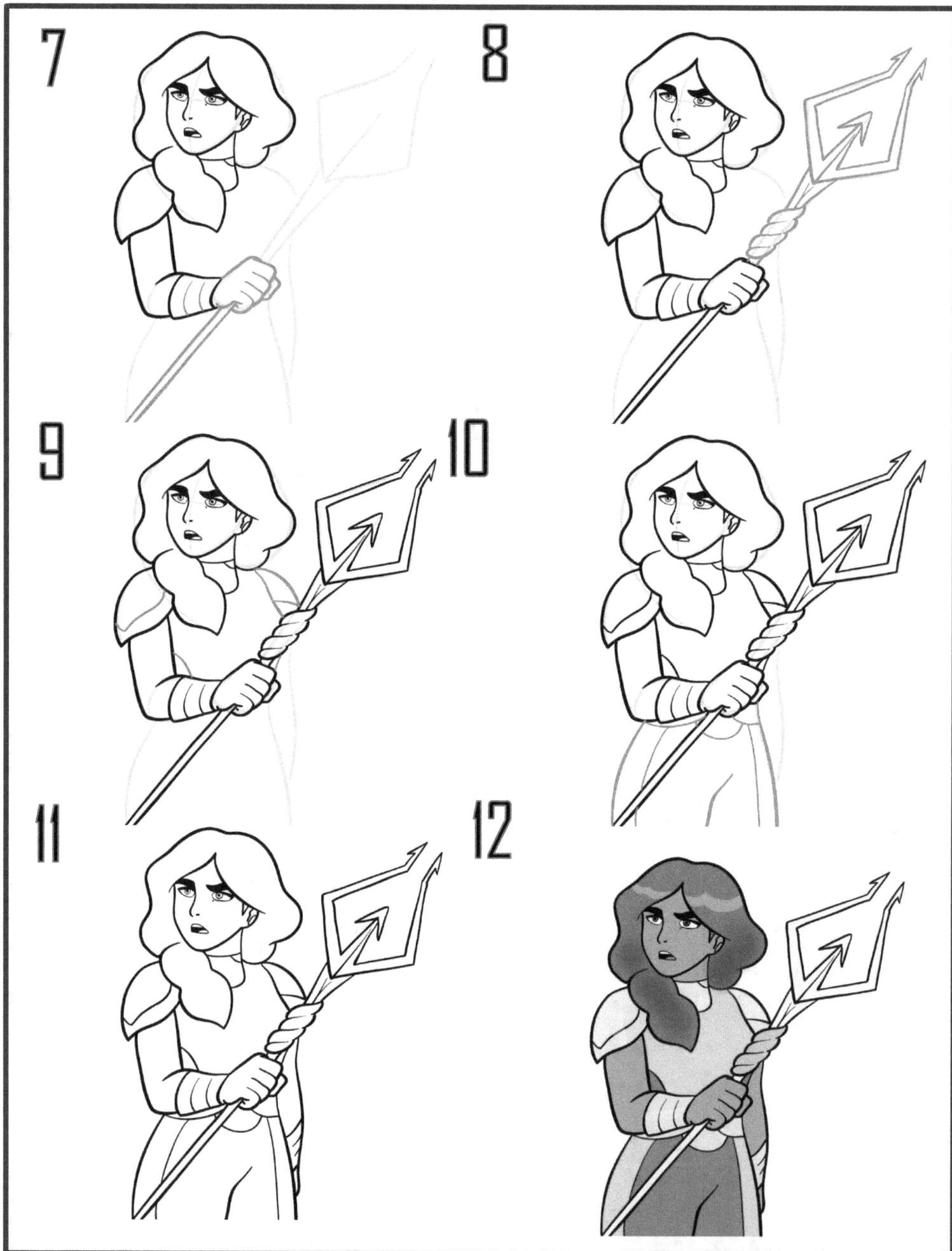

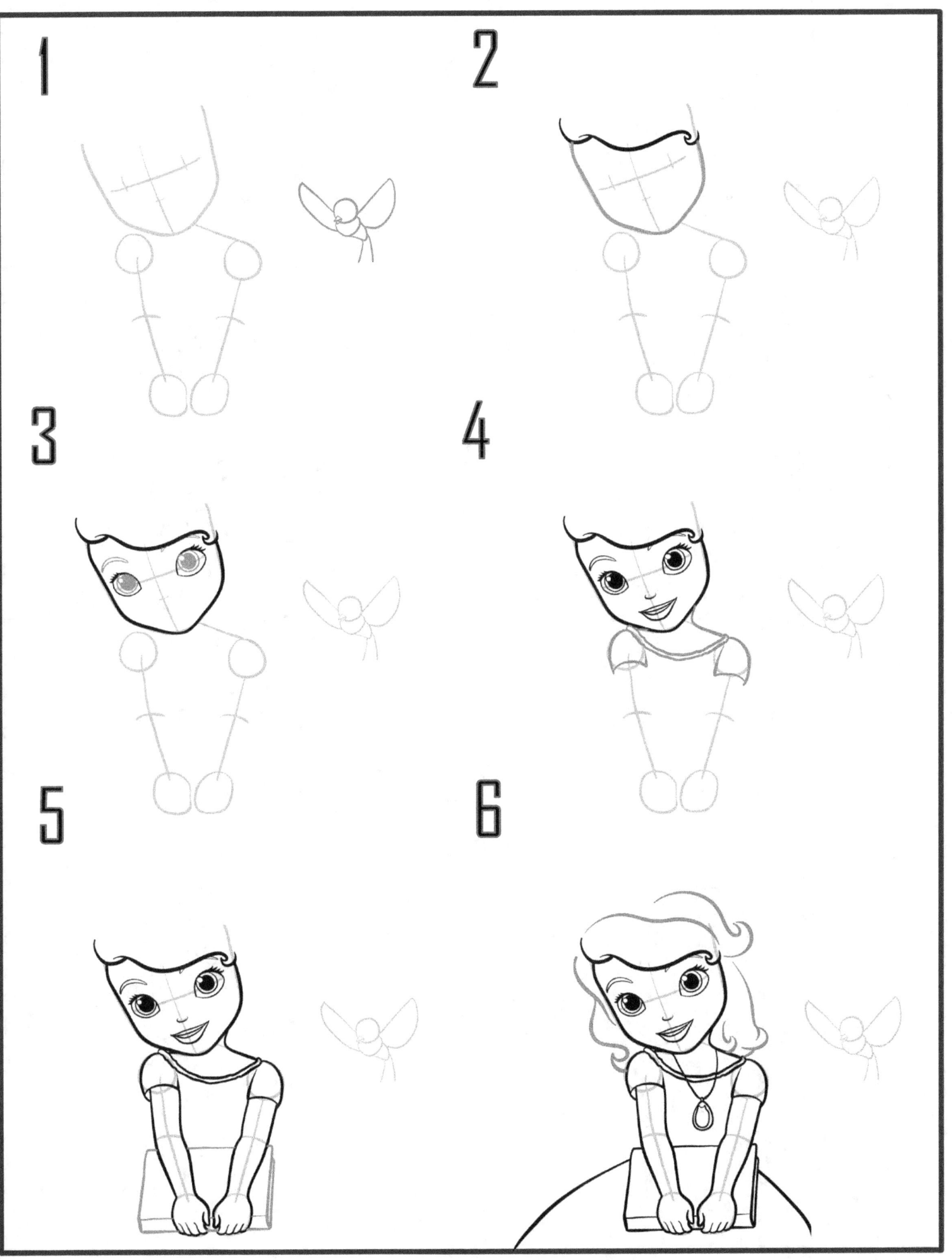

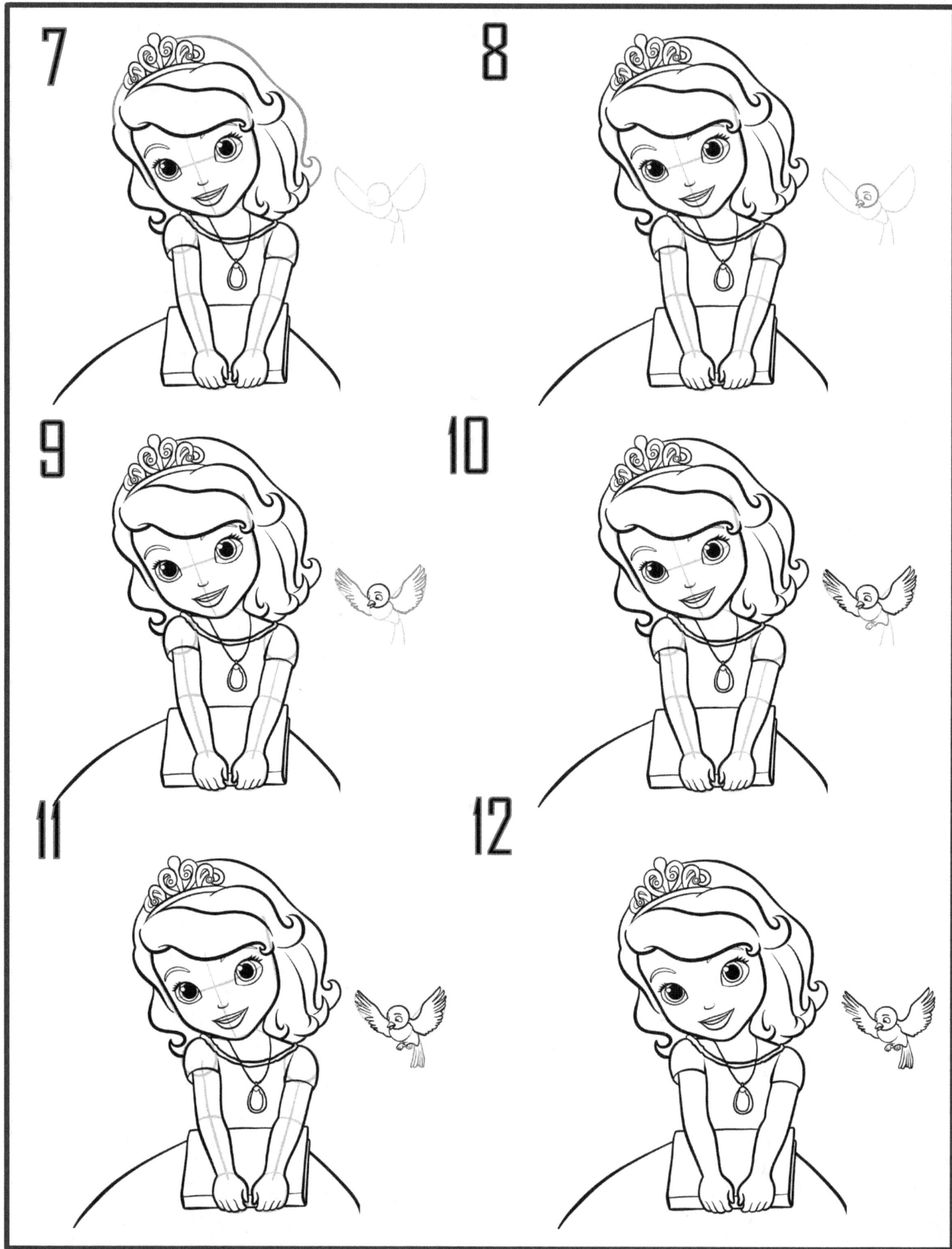

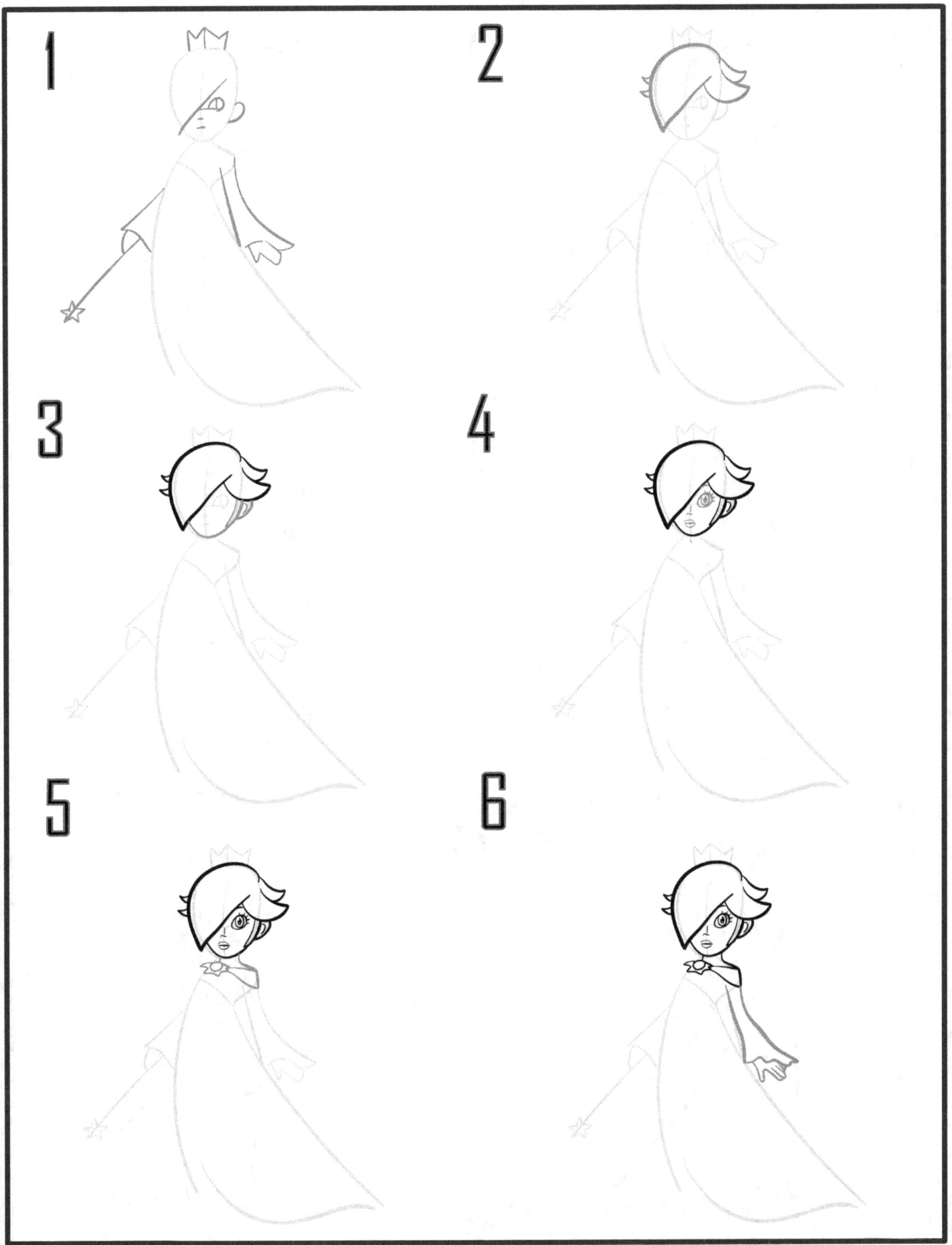

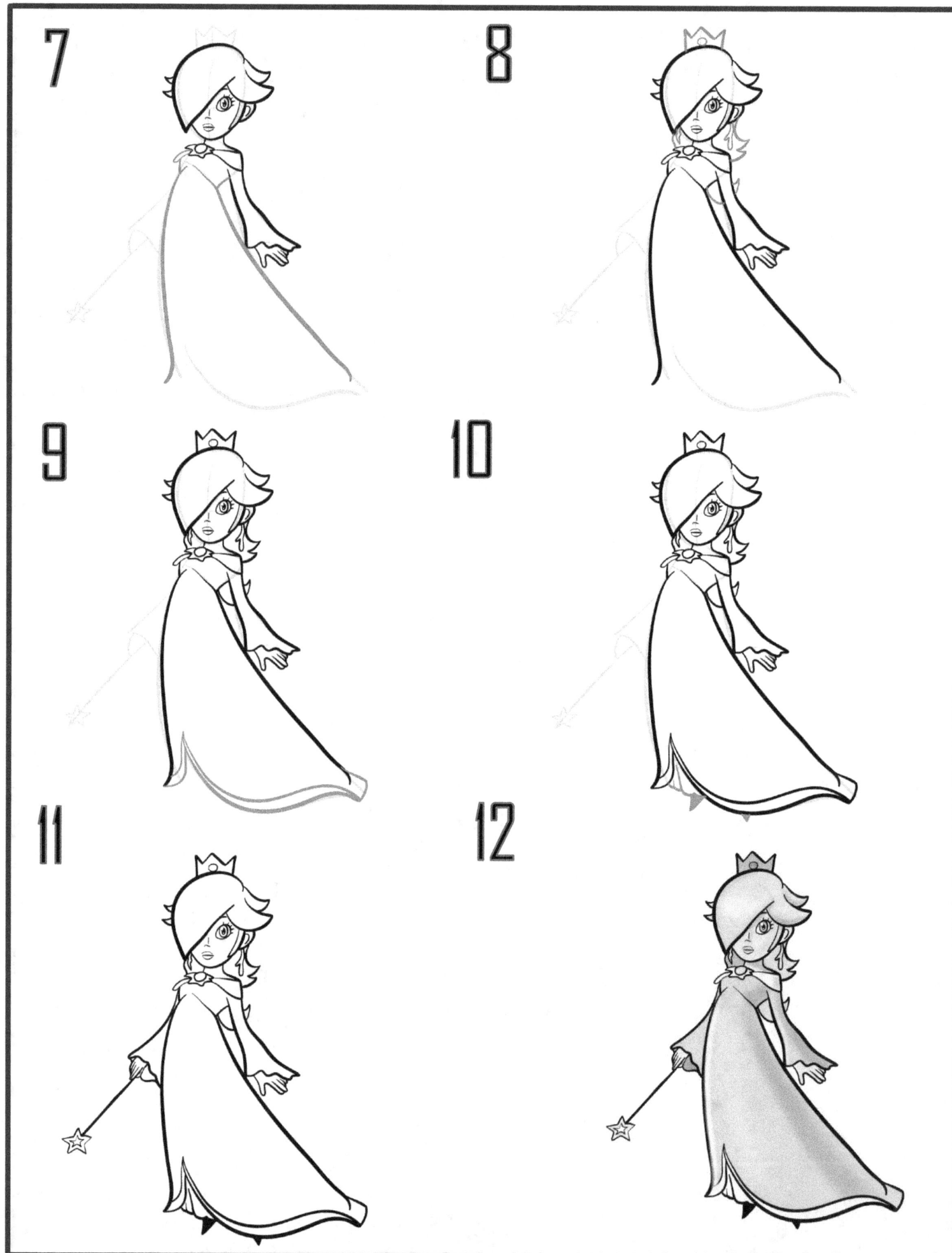

1

2

3

4

5

6

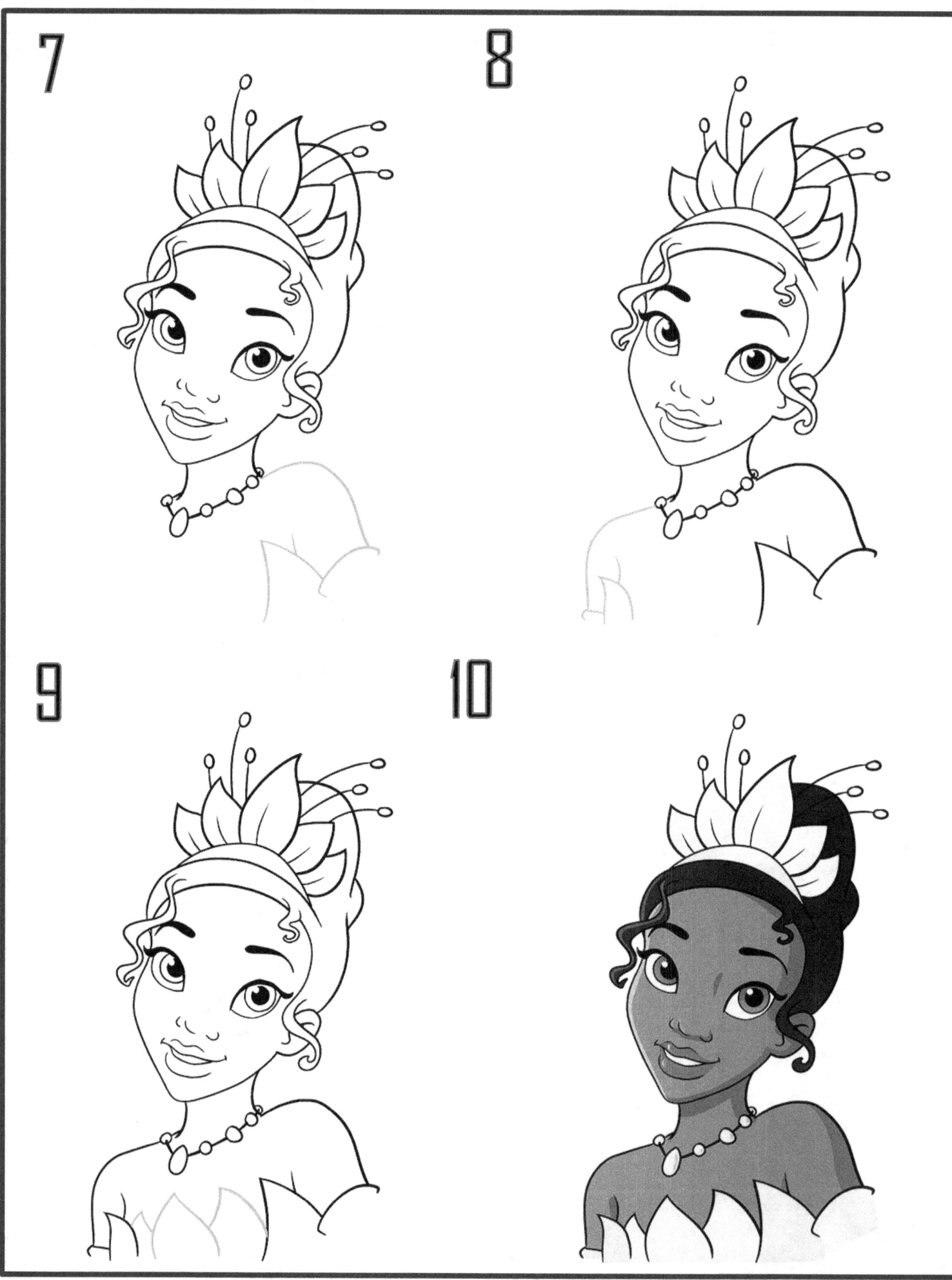

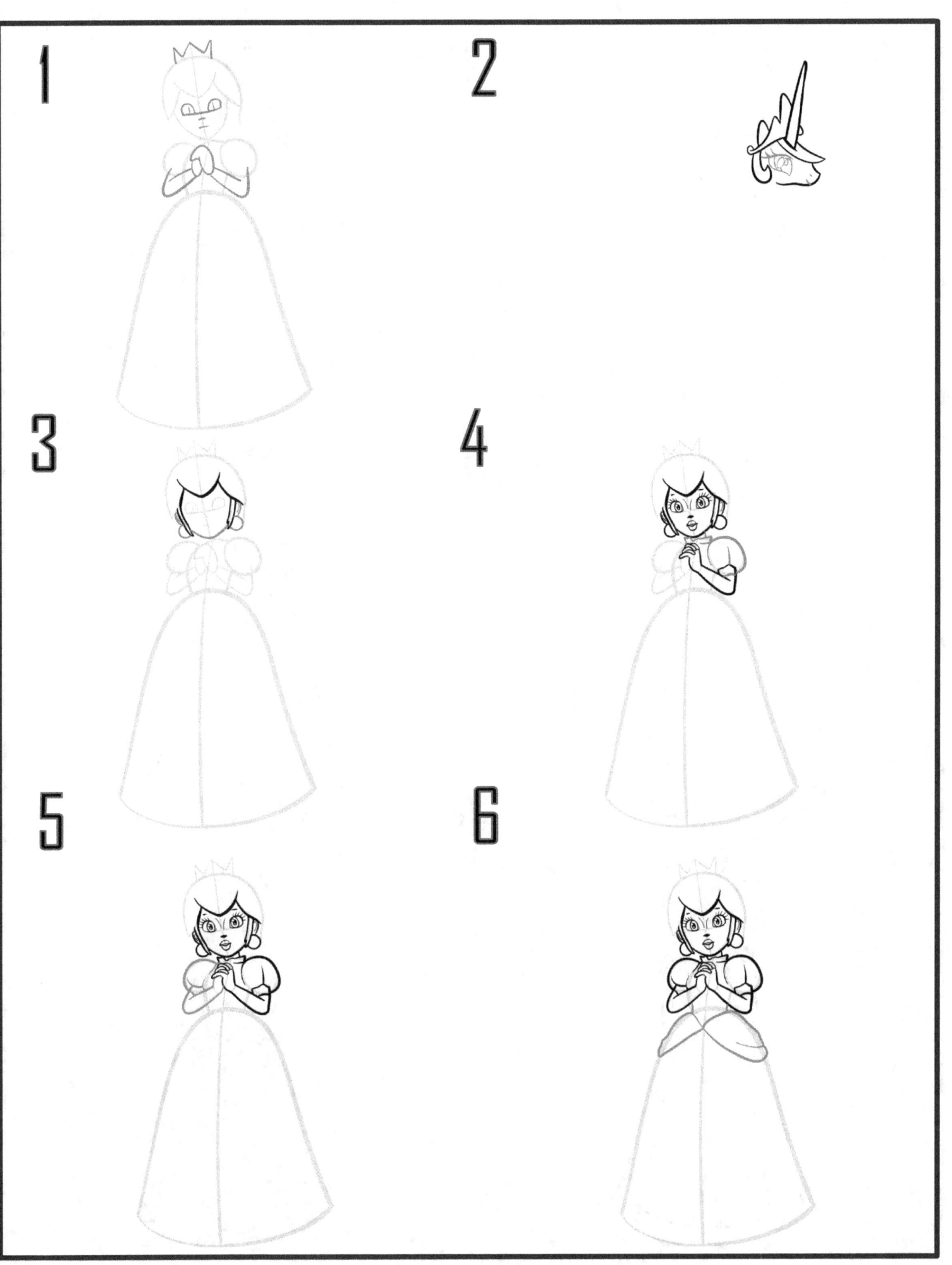

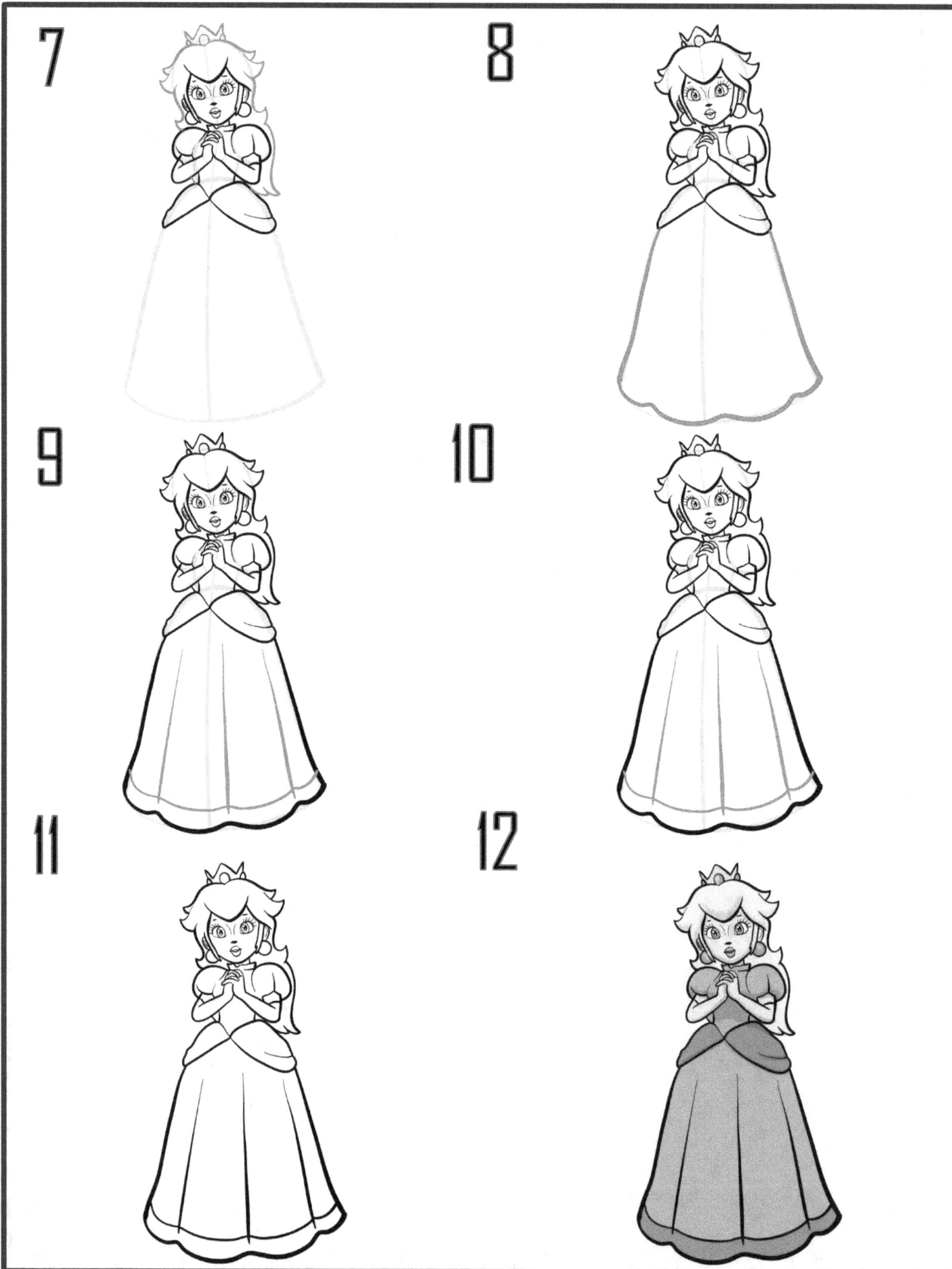

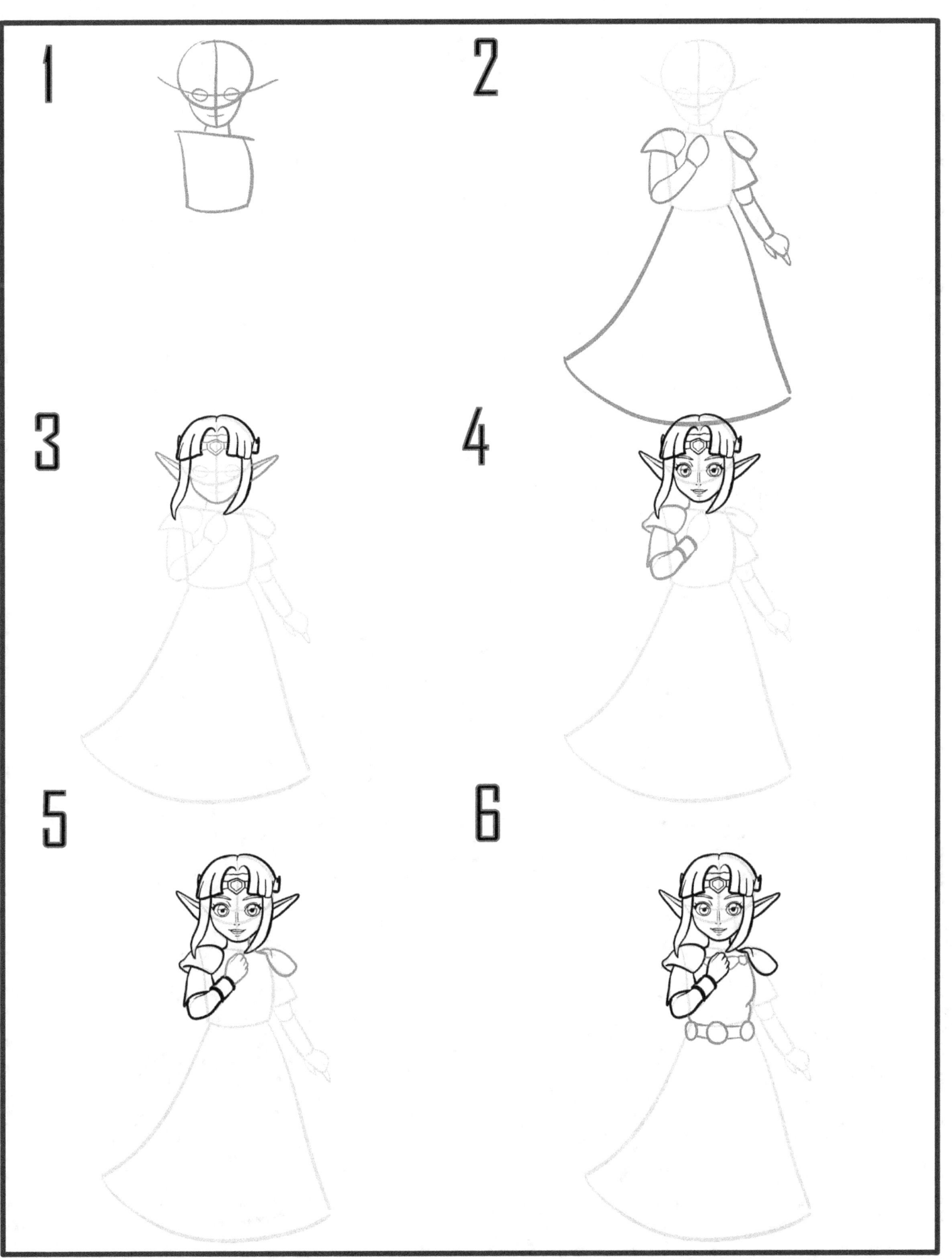

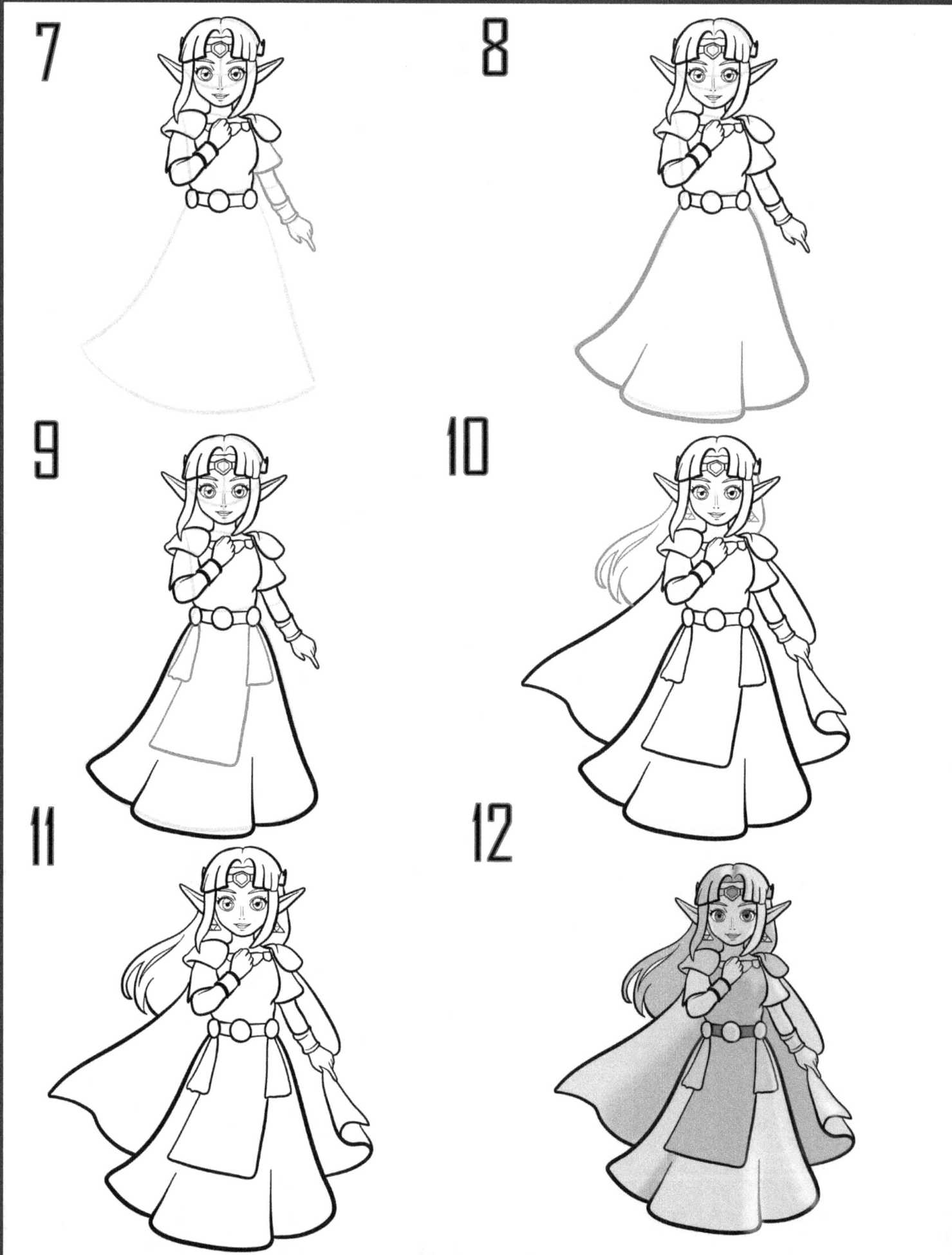

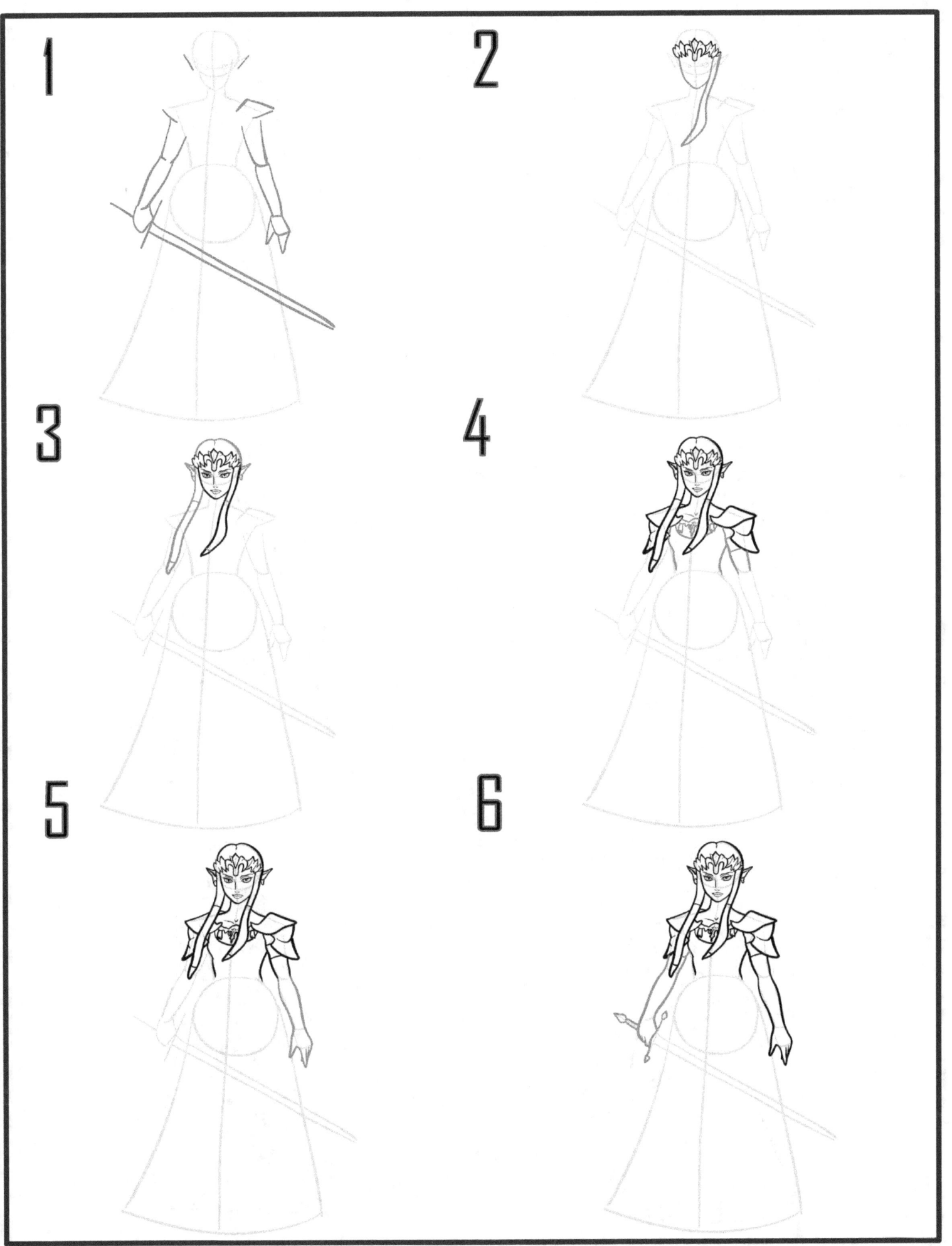

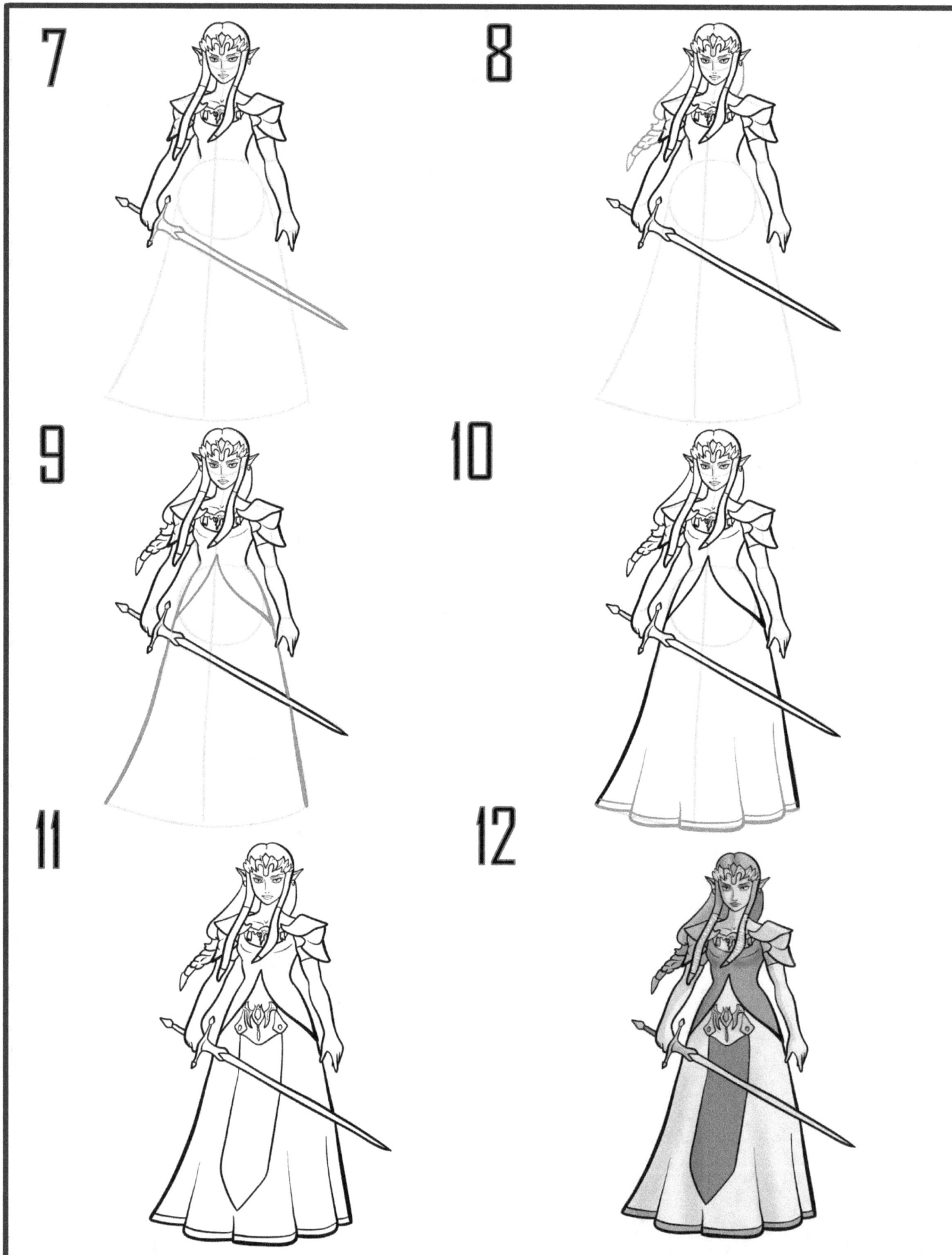

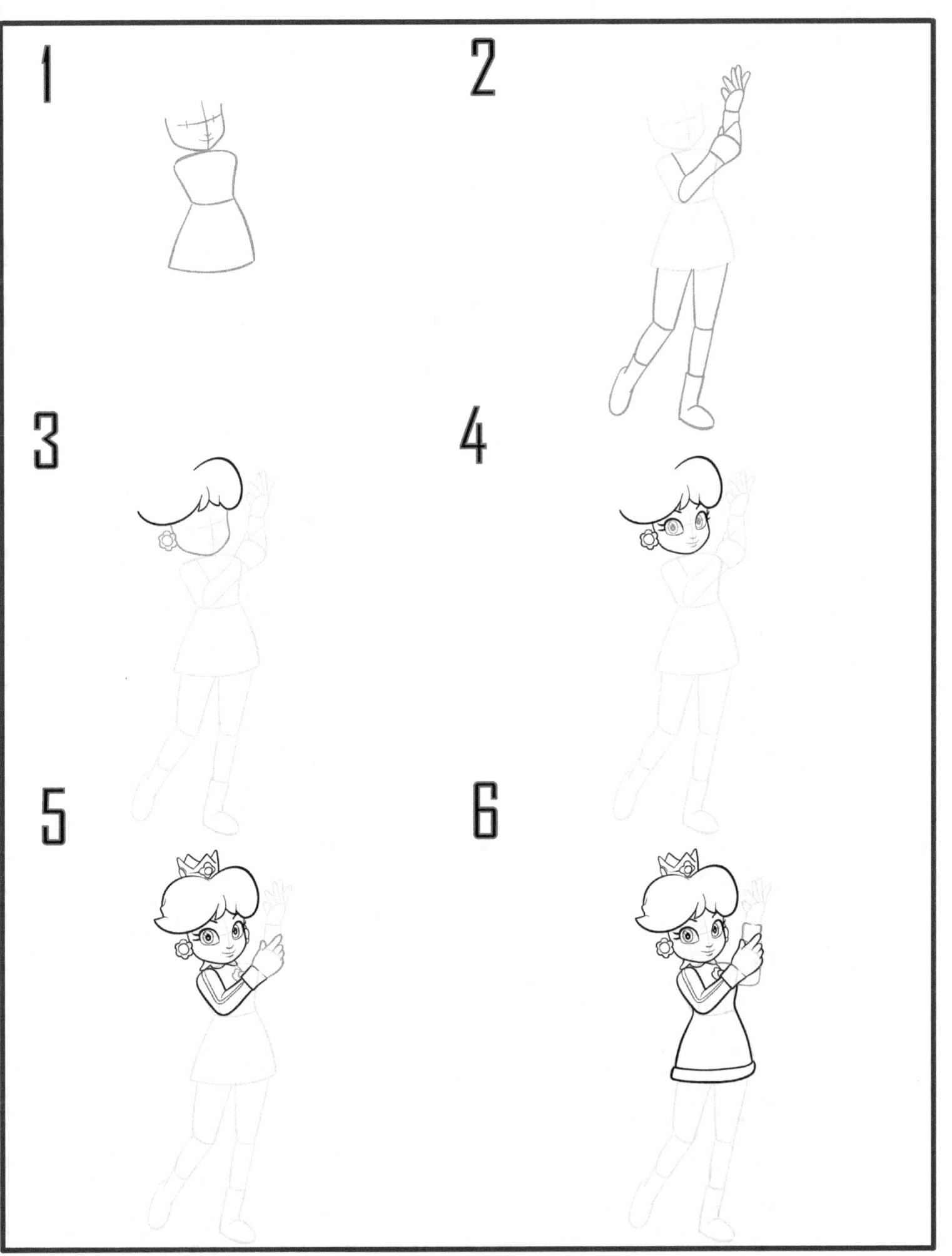

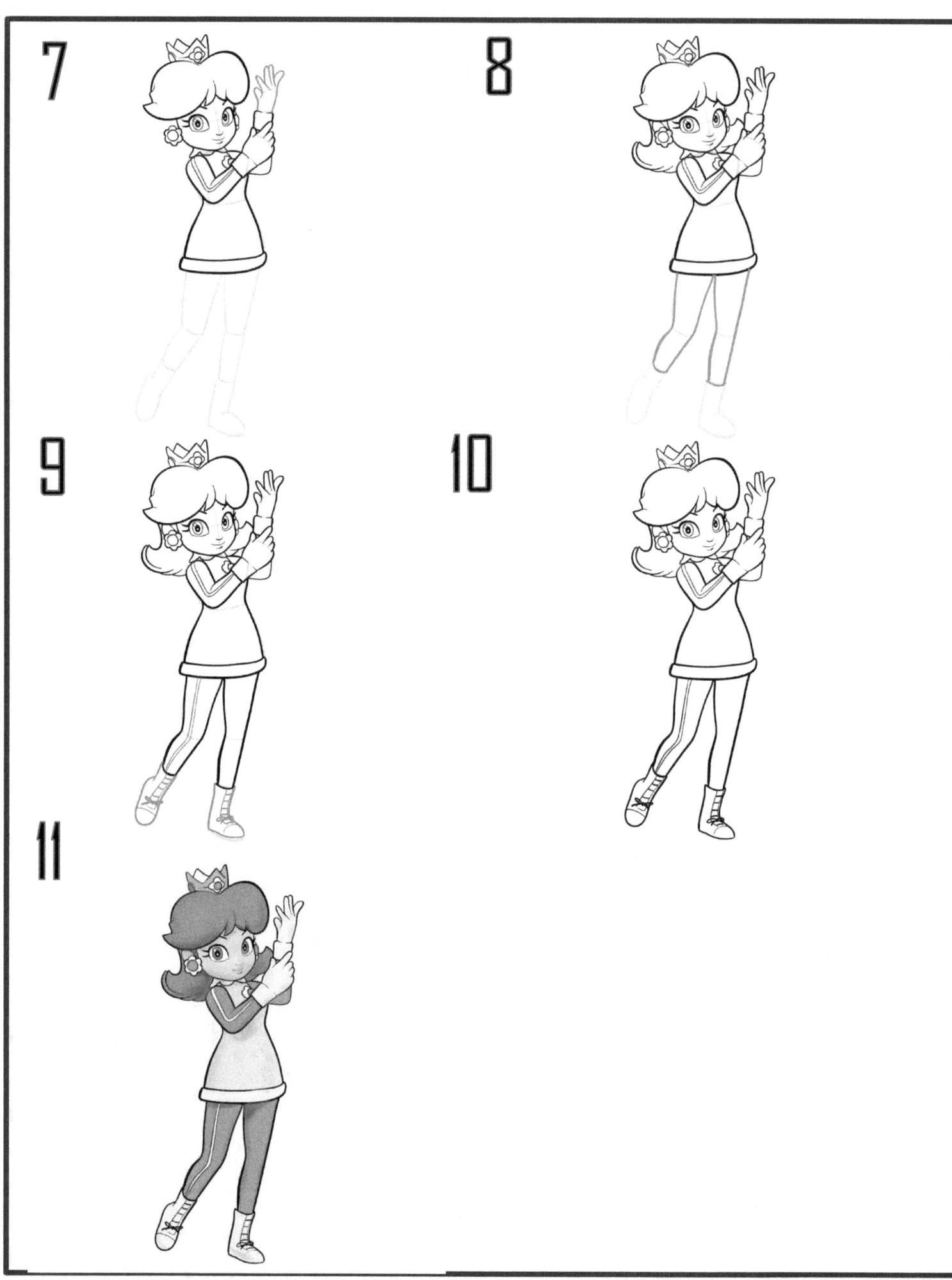

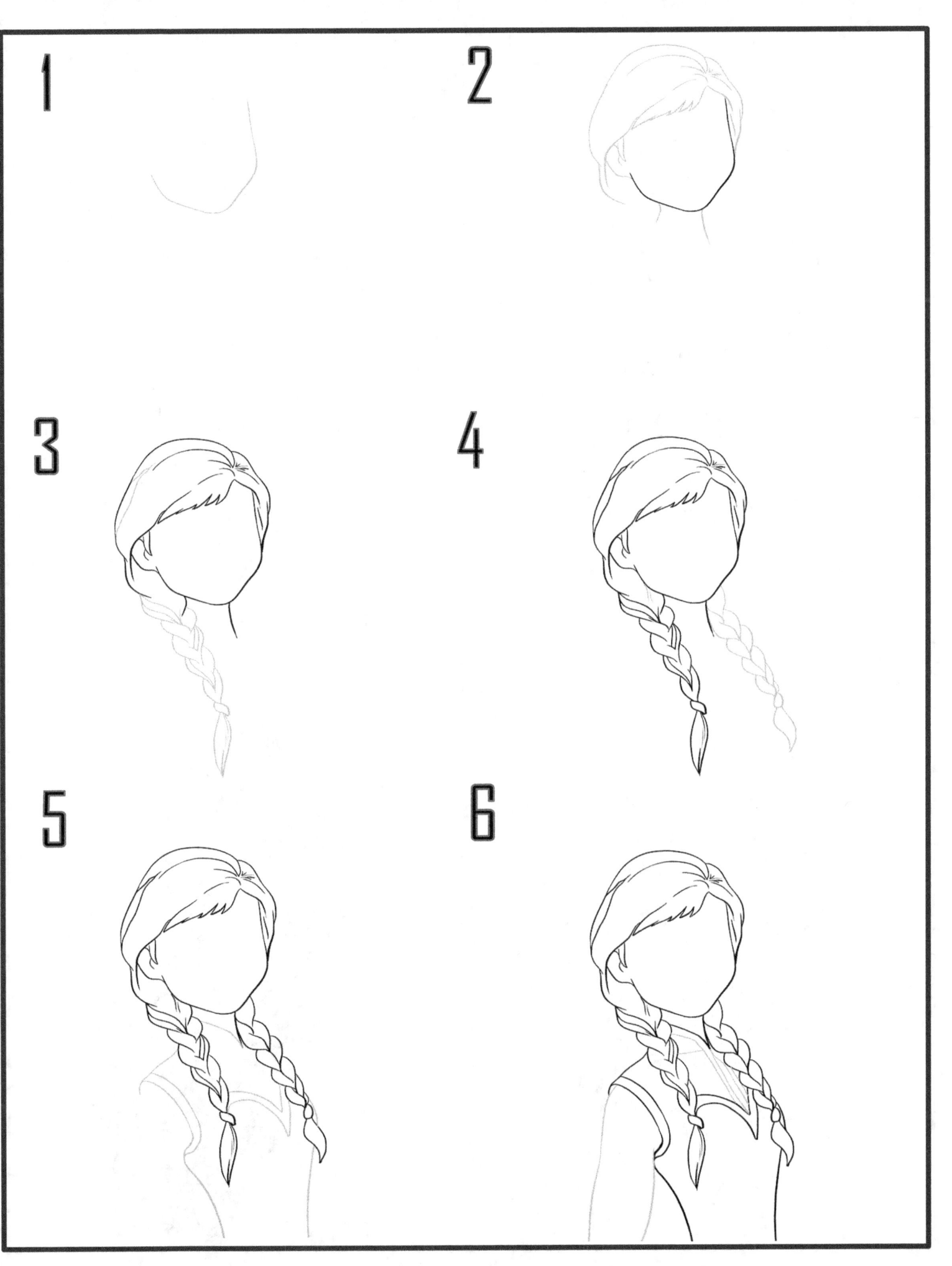

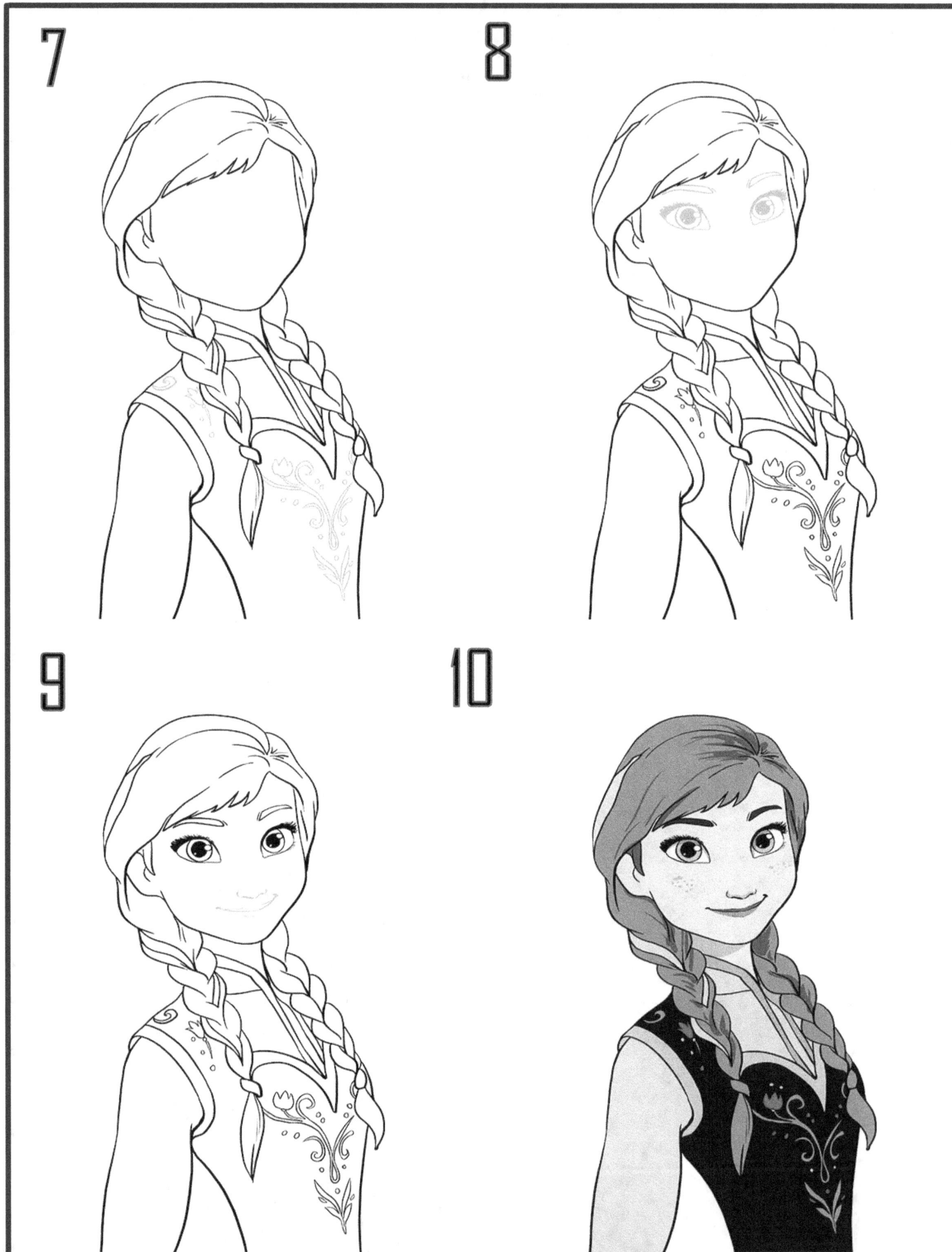

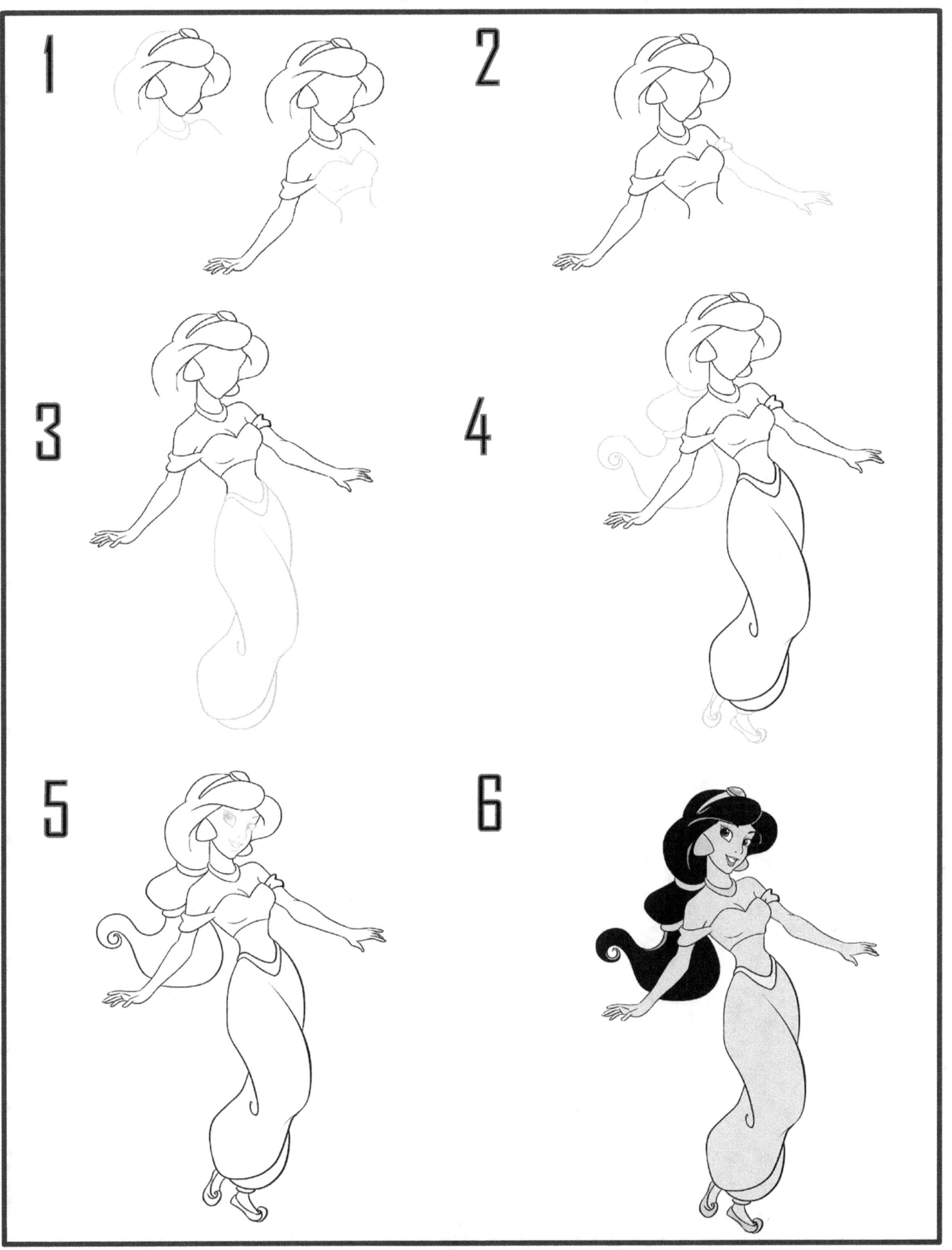

1

2

3

4

5

6

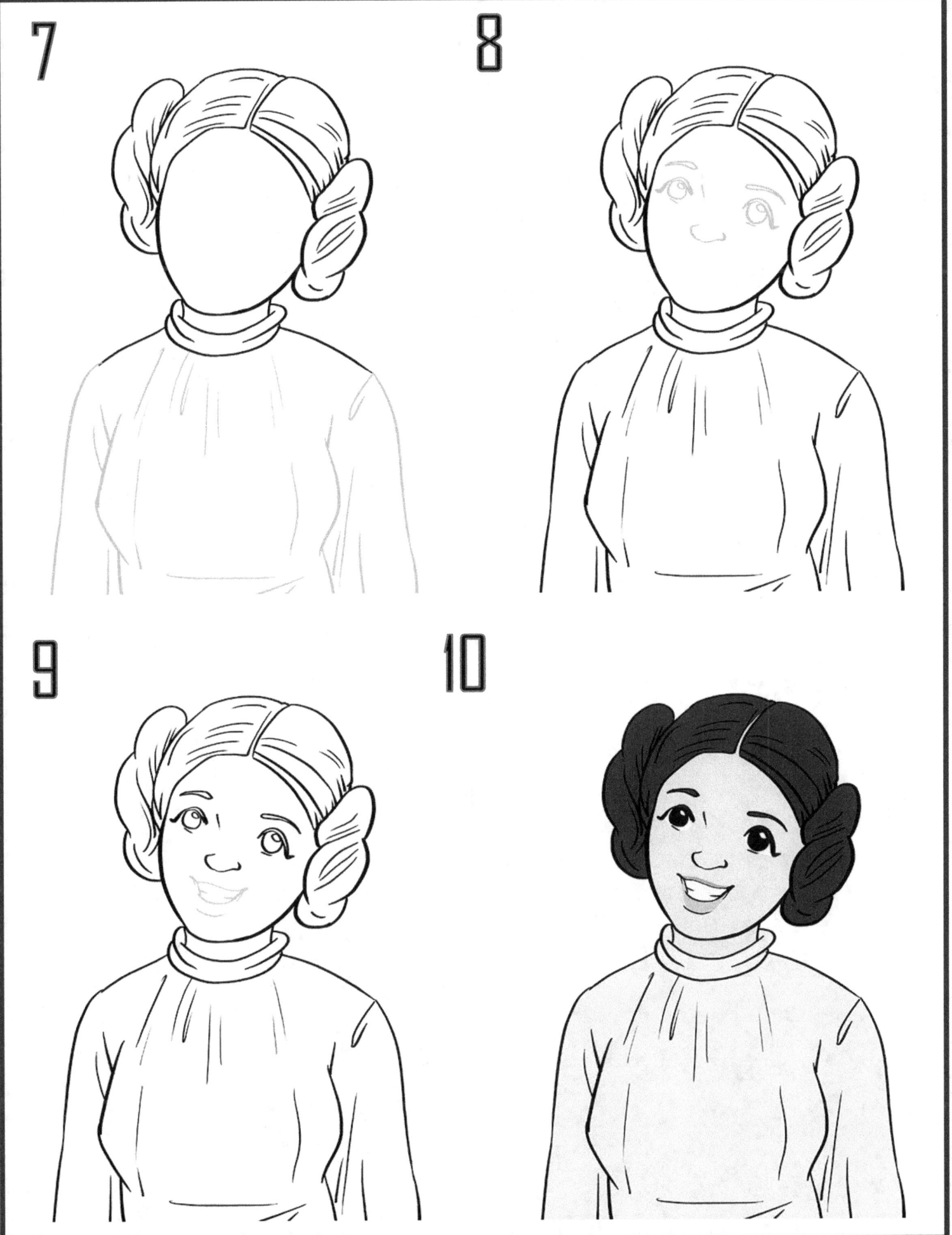

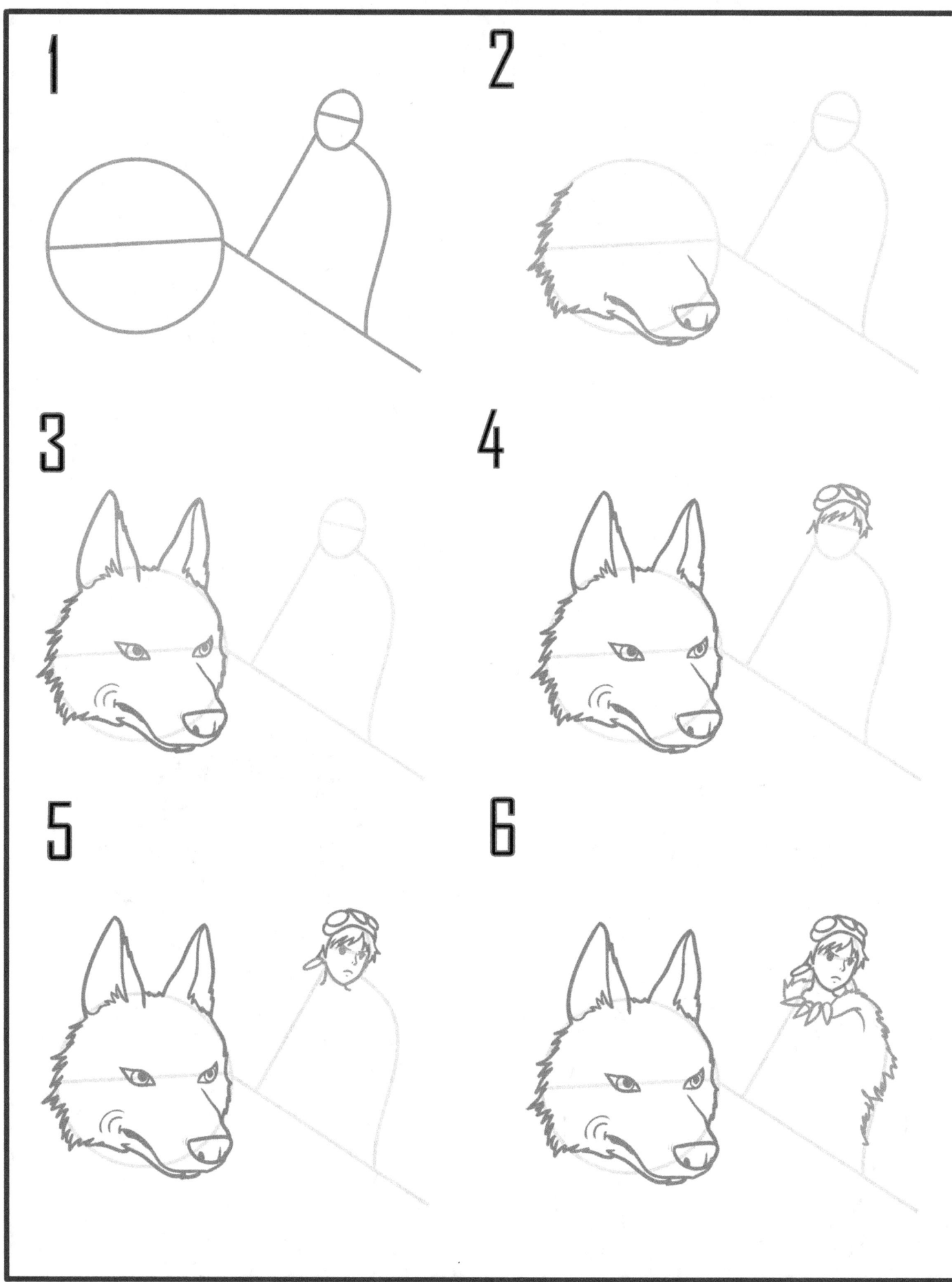

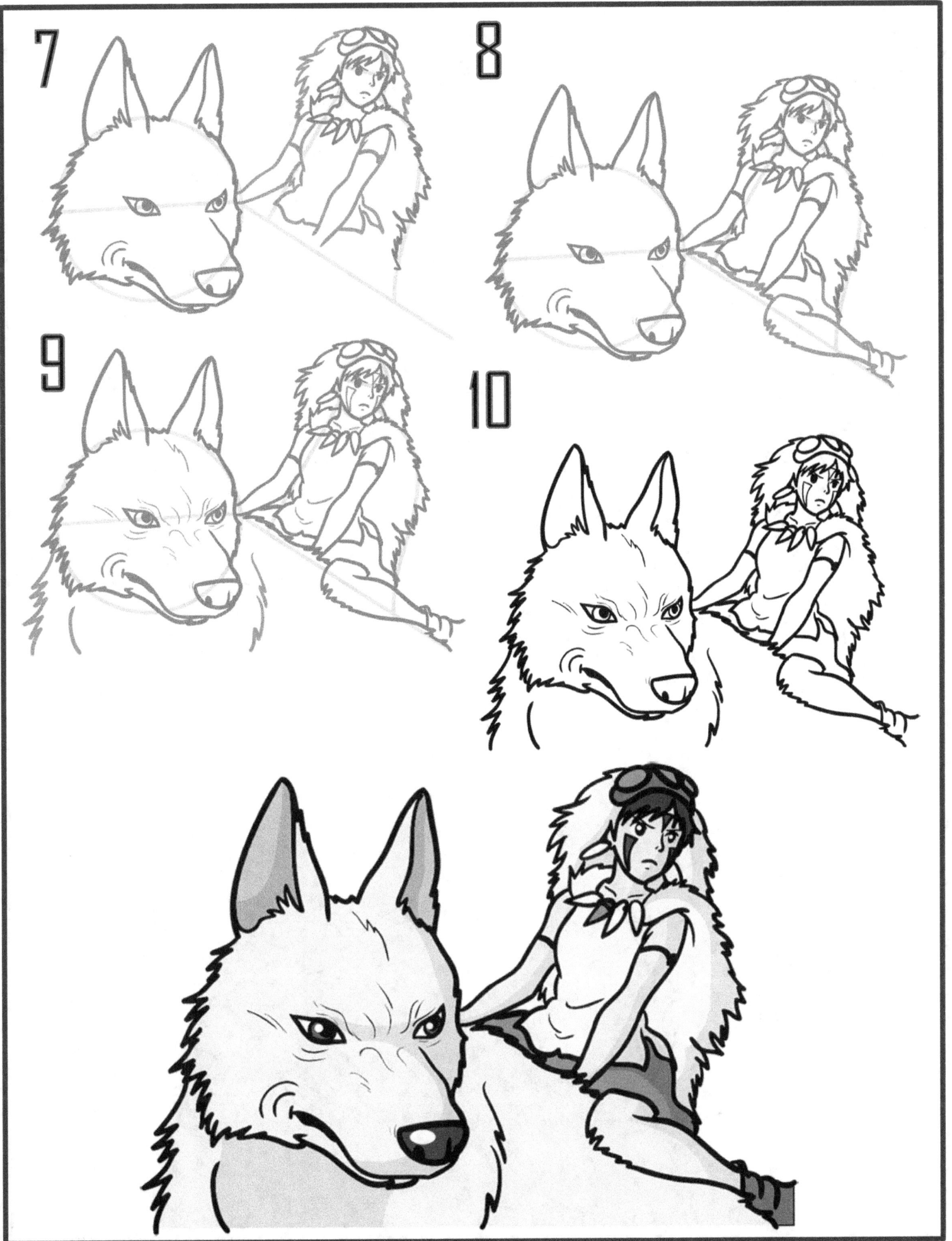

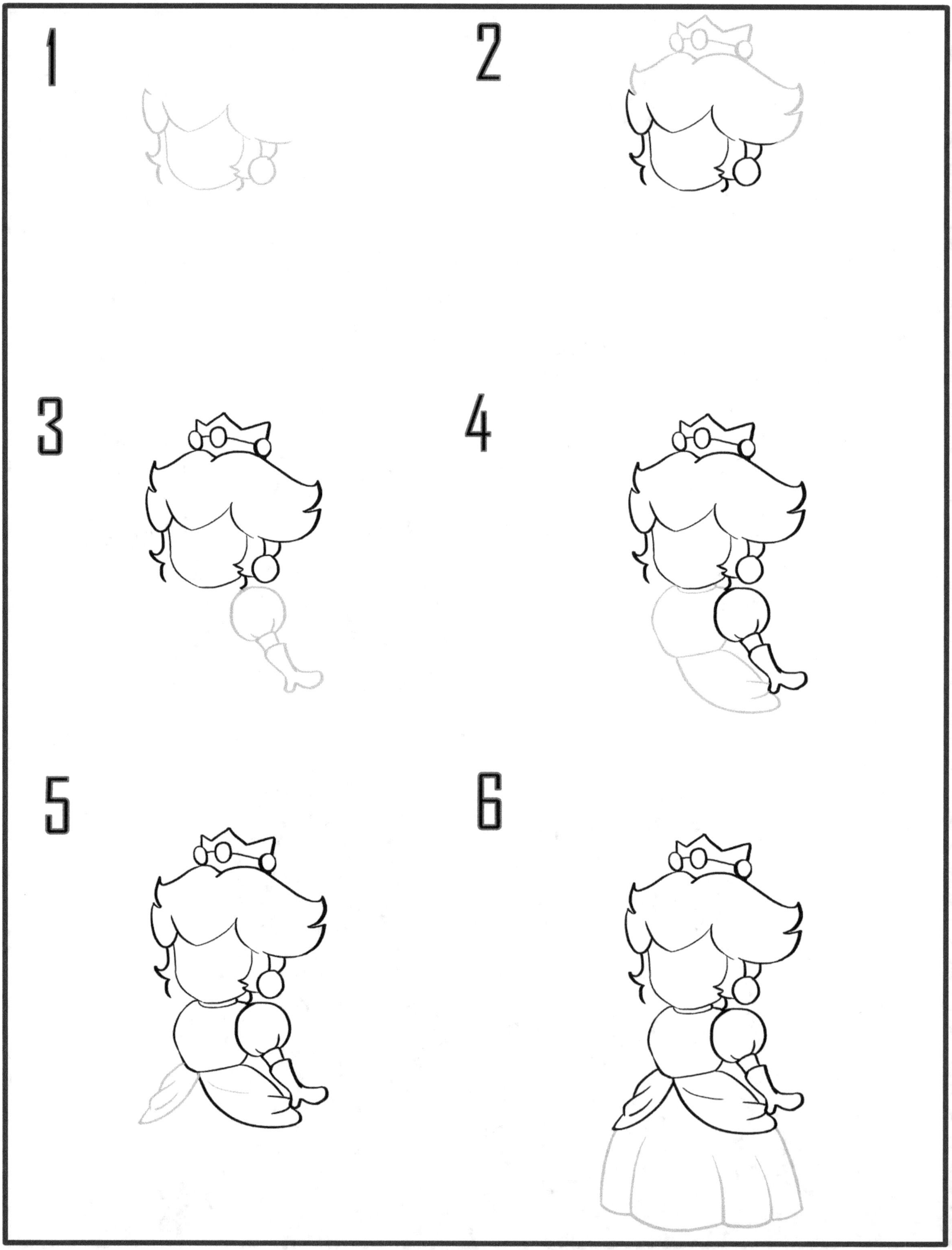
1
2
3
4
5
6

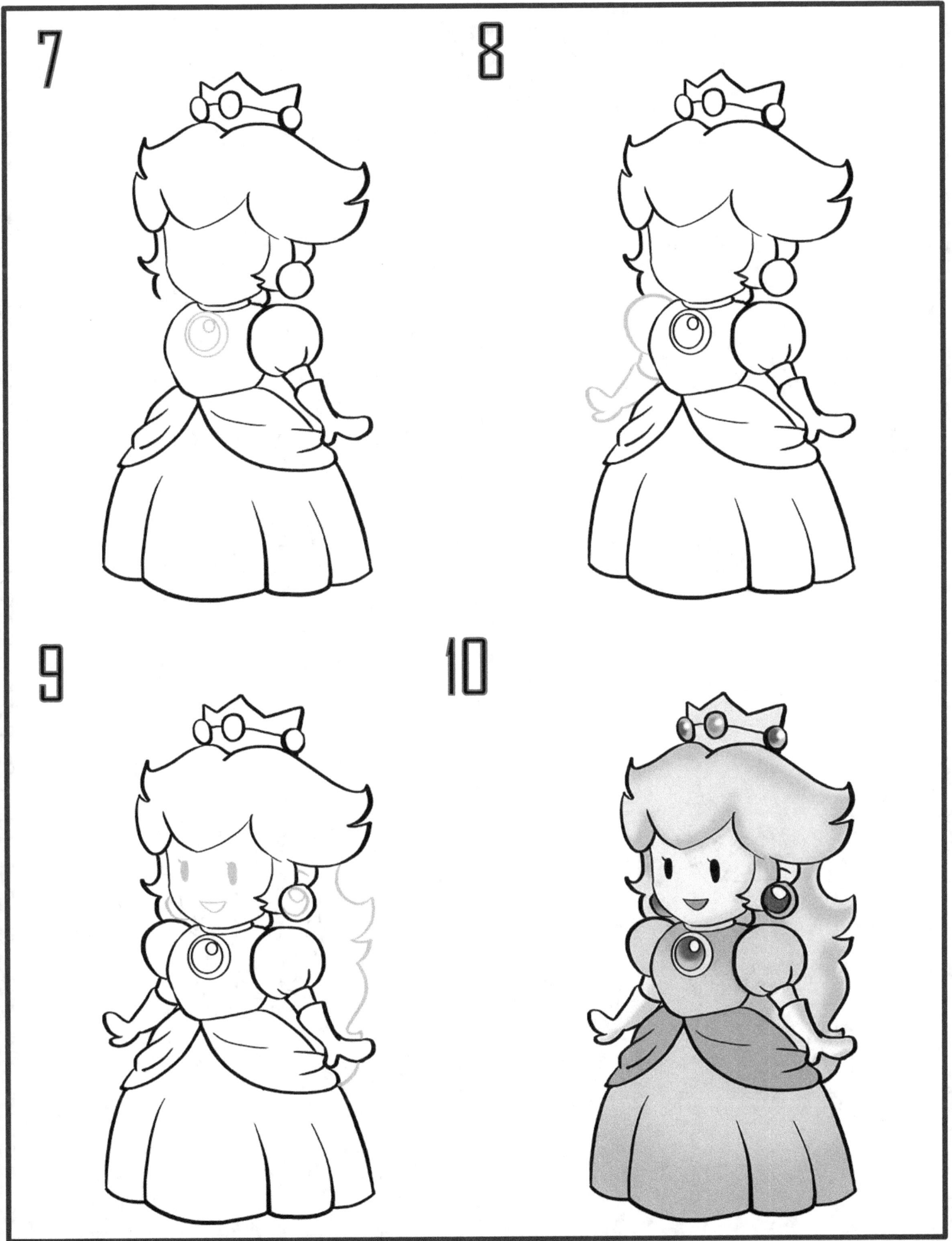

1

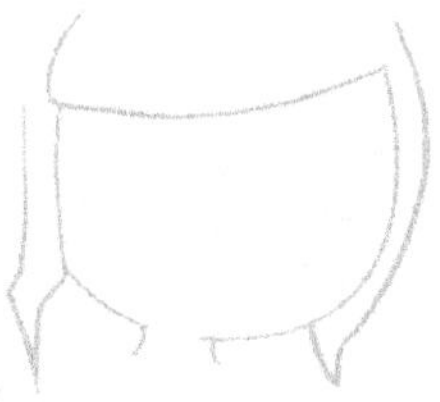

2

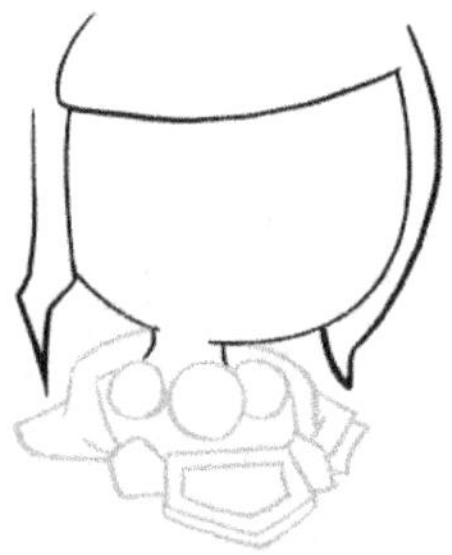

3

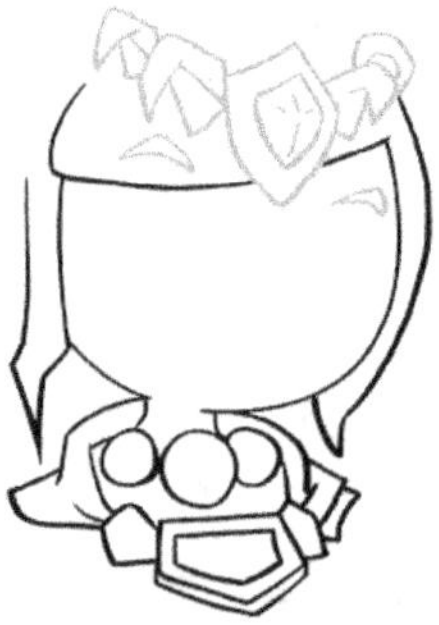

4

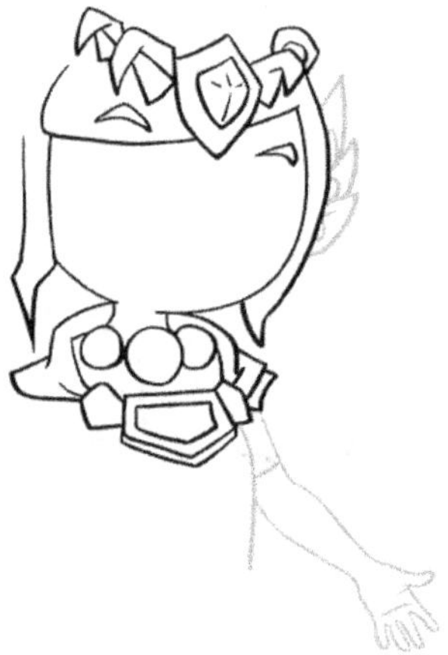

5

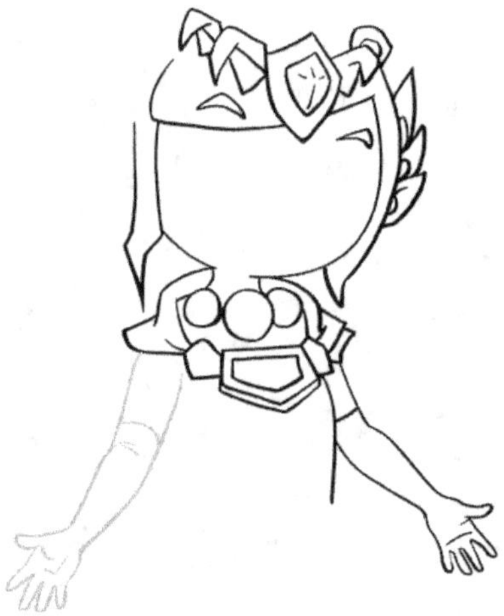

6

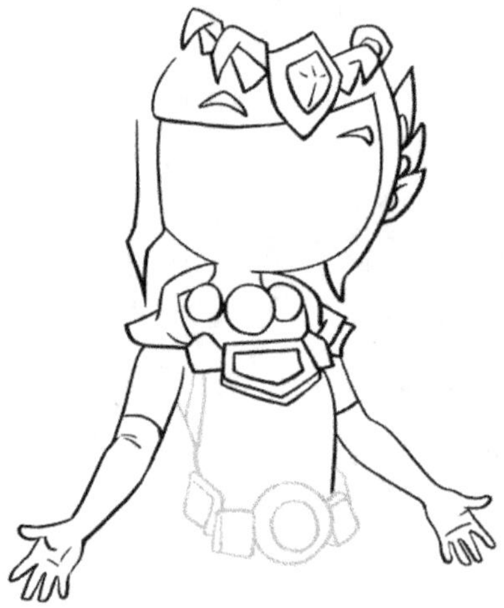

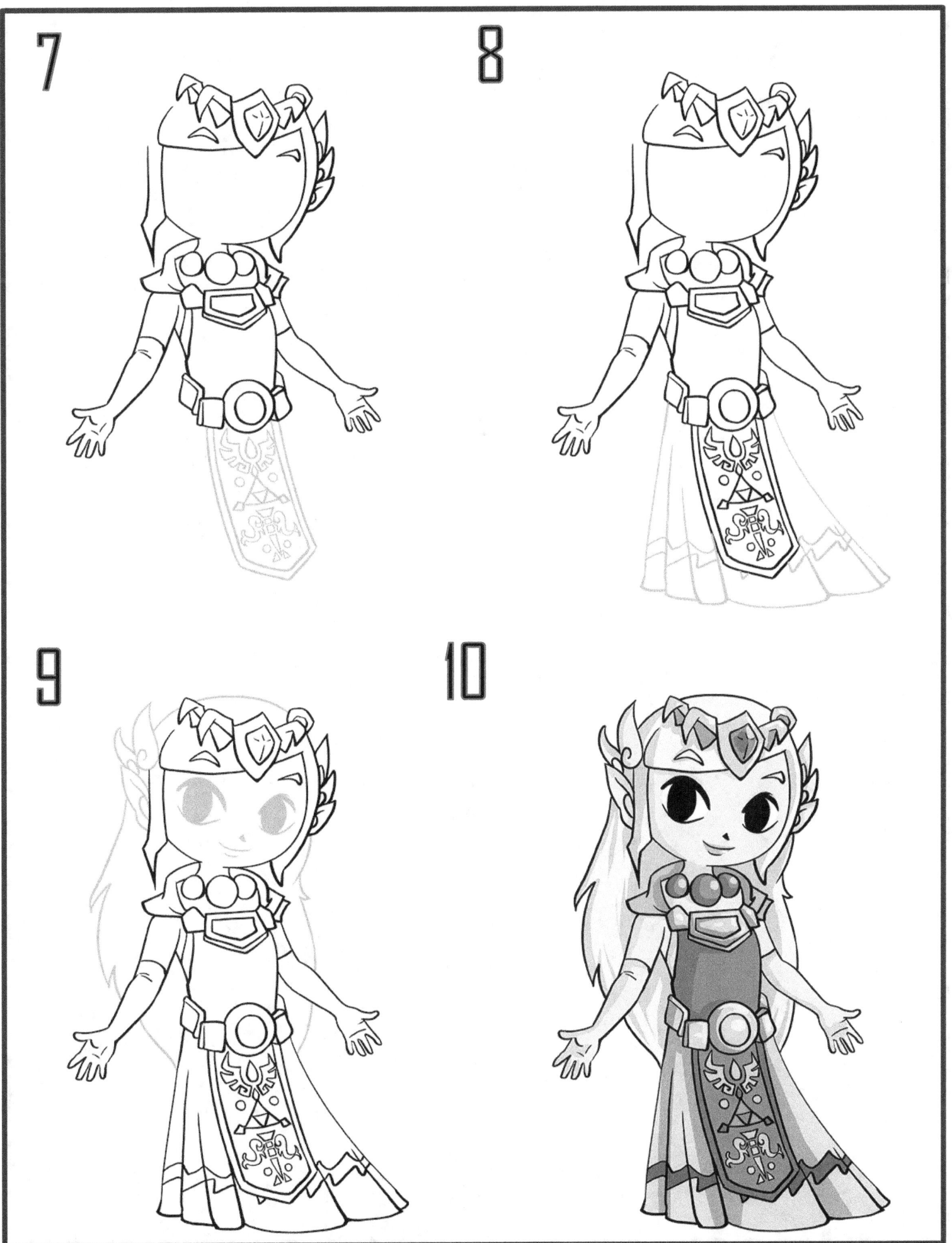

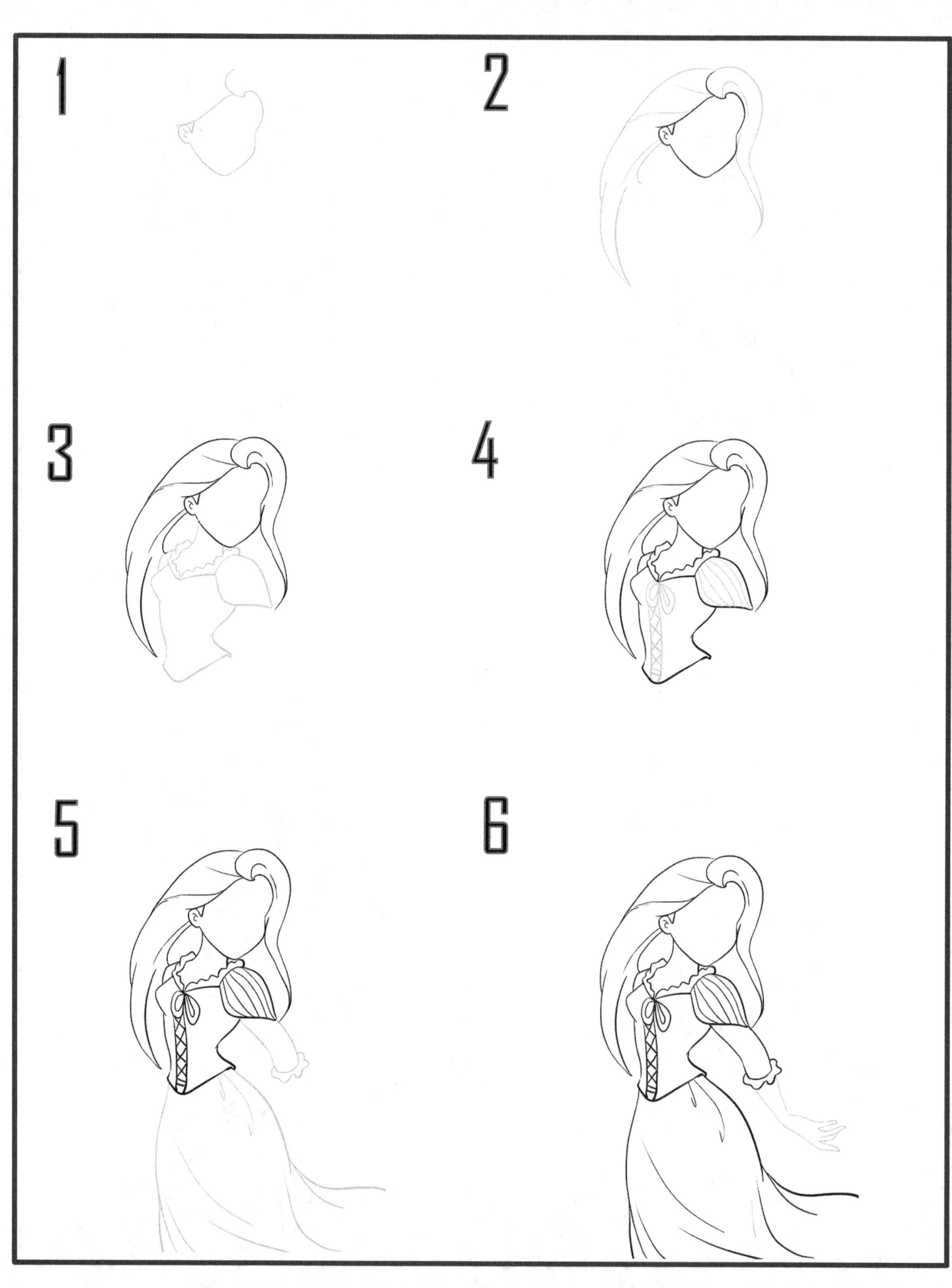

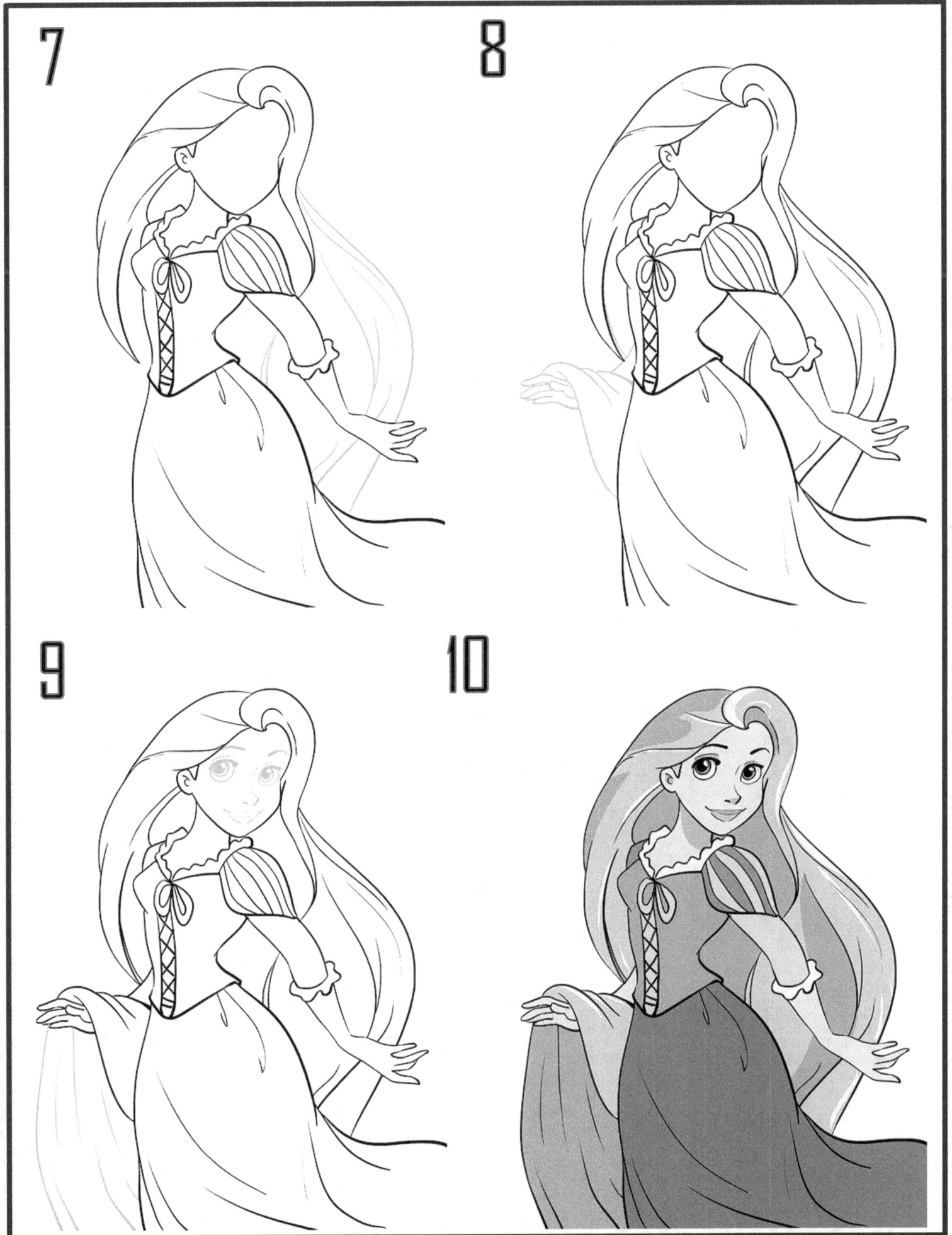

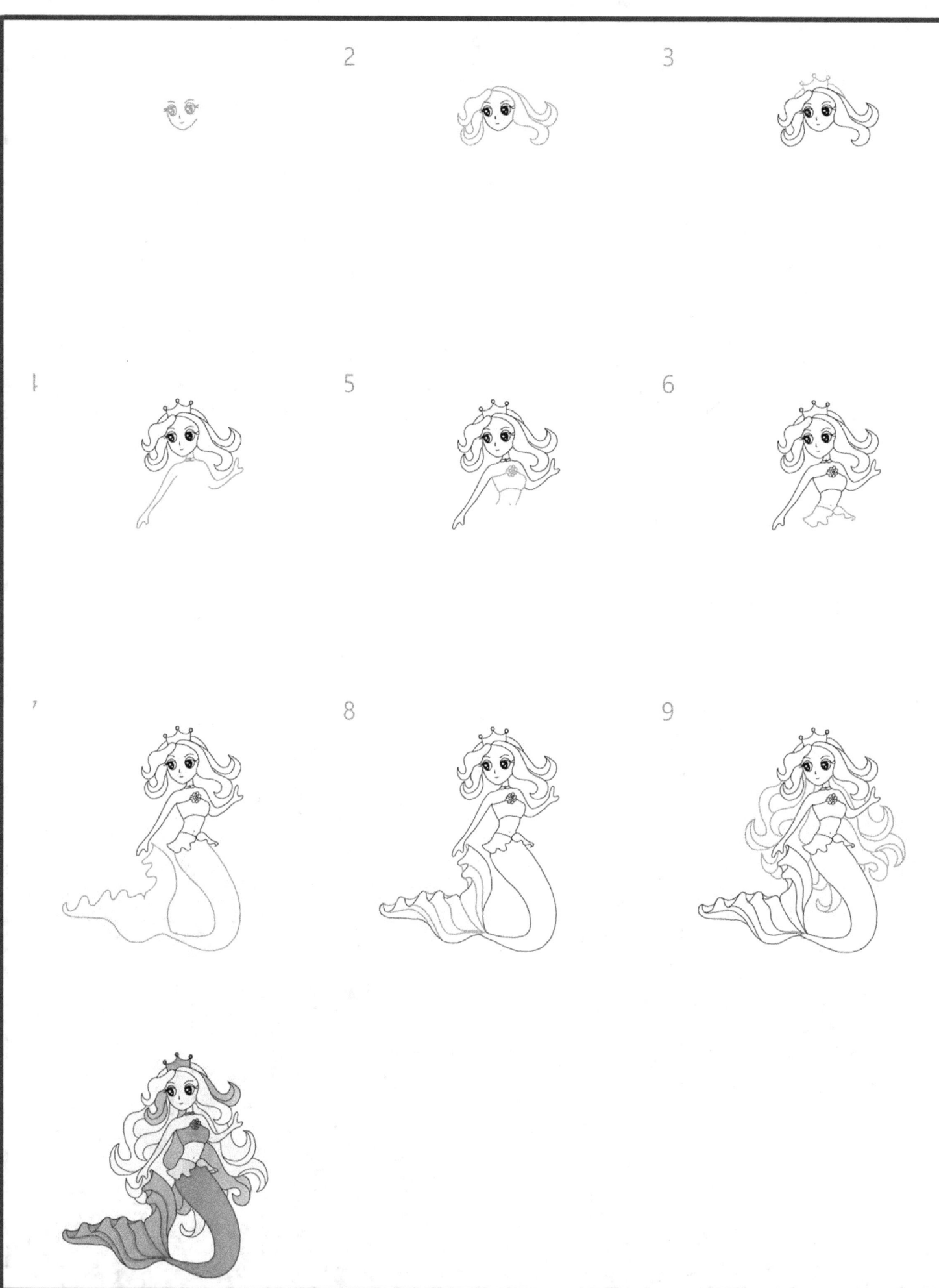

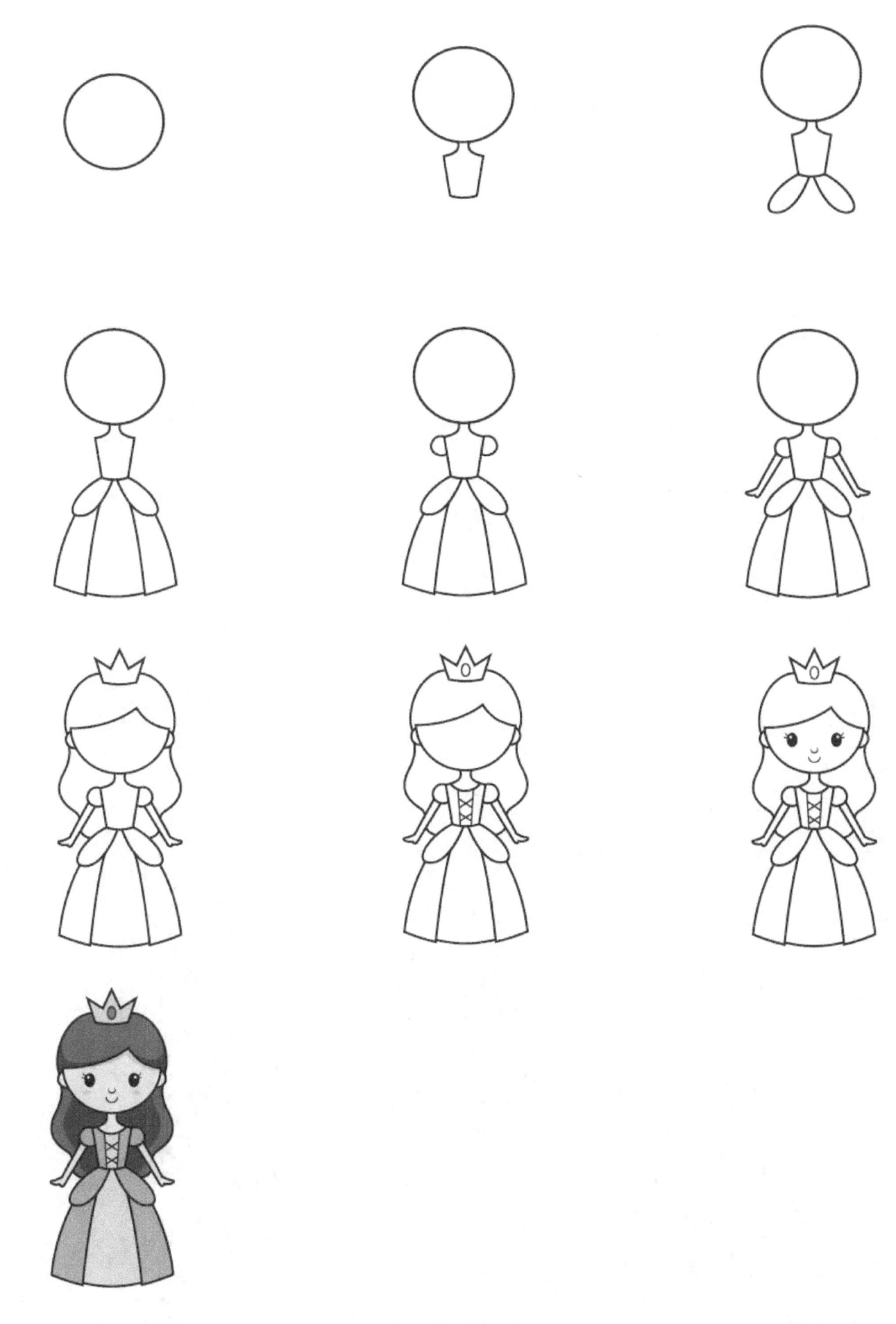

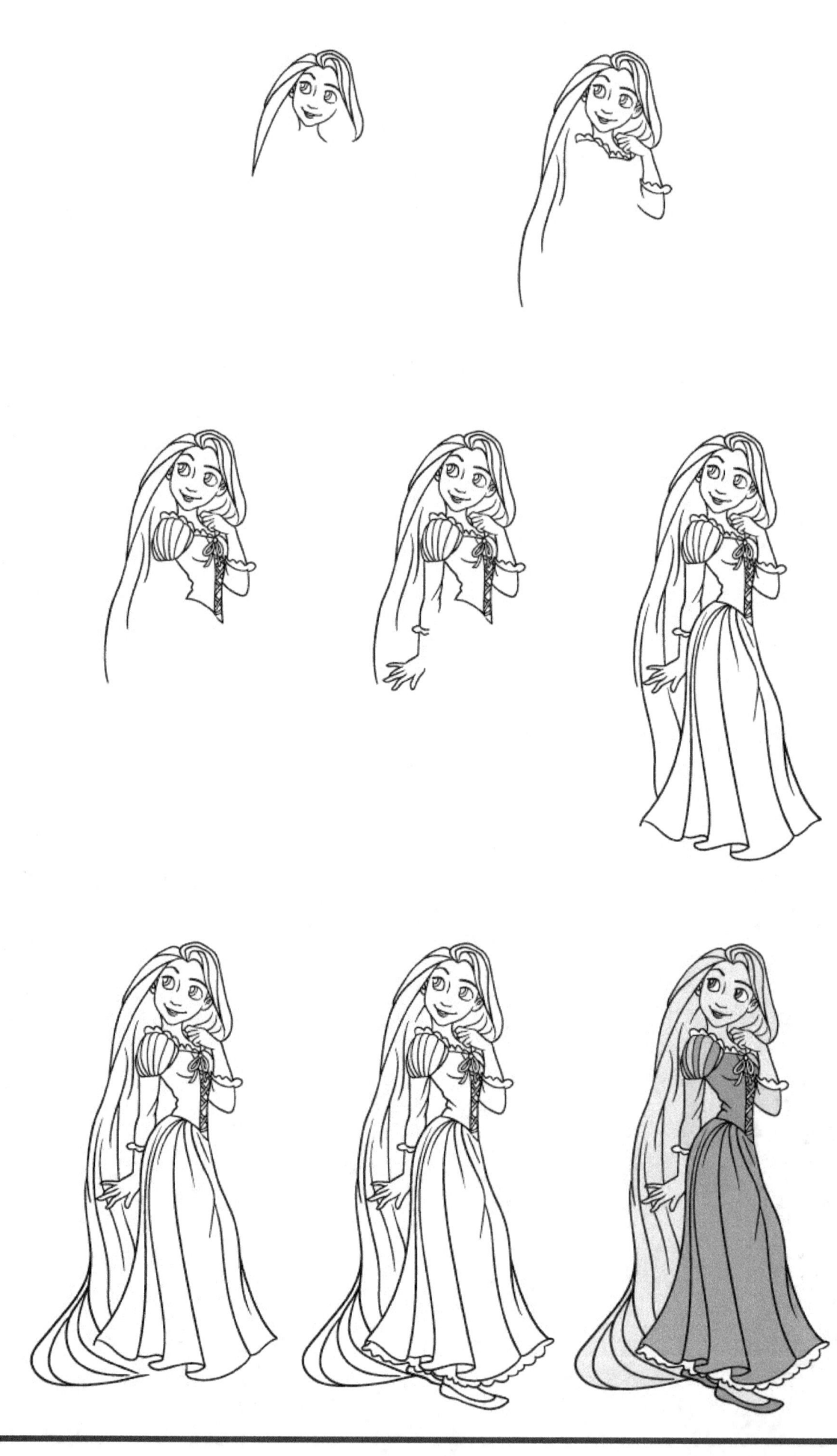

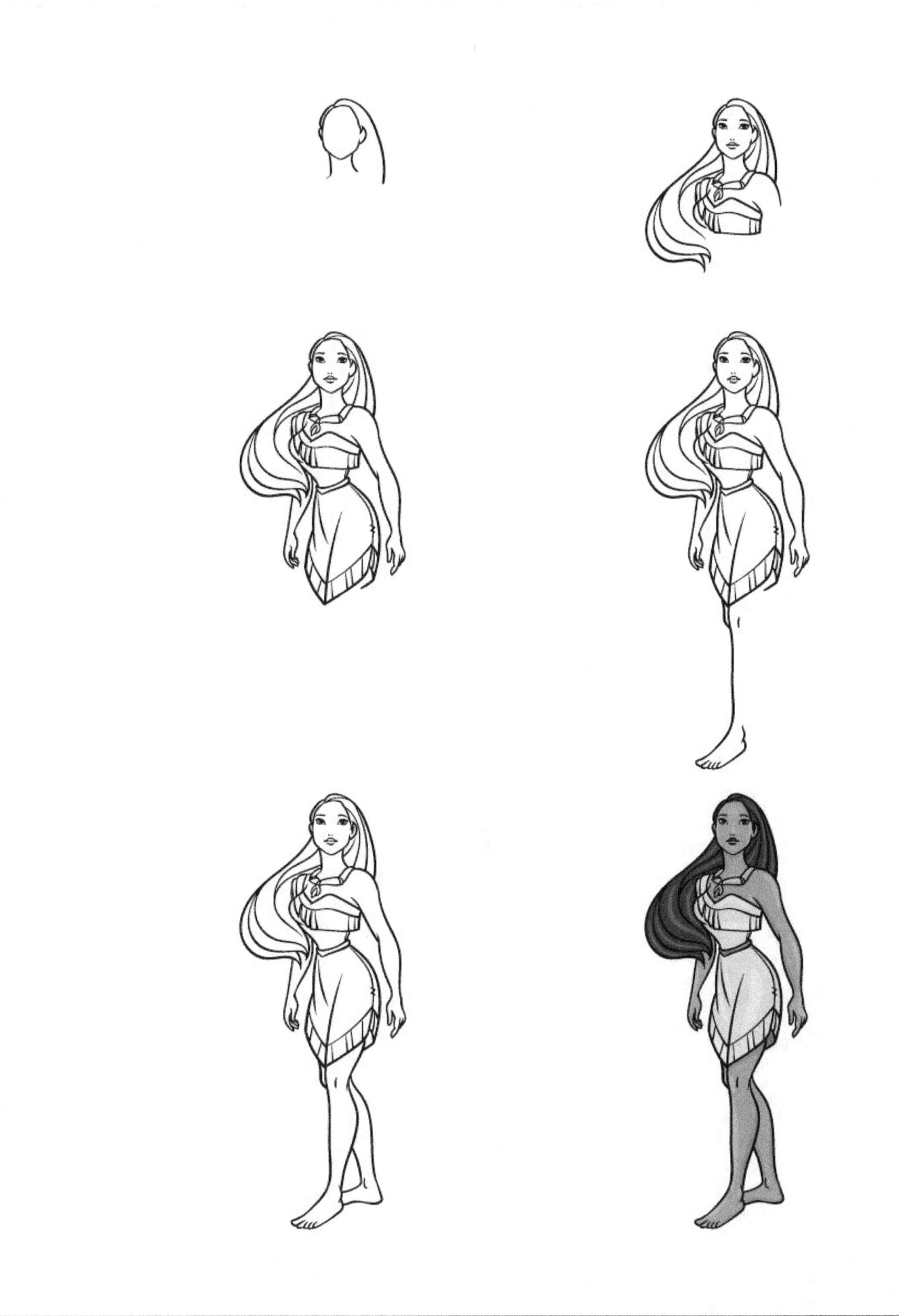

1

2

3

4

5

6

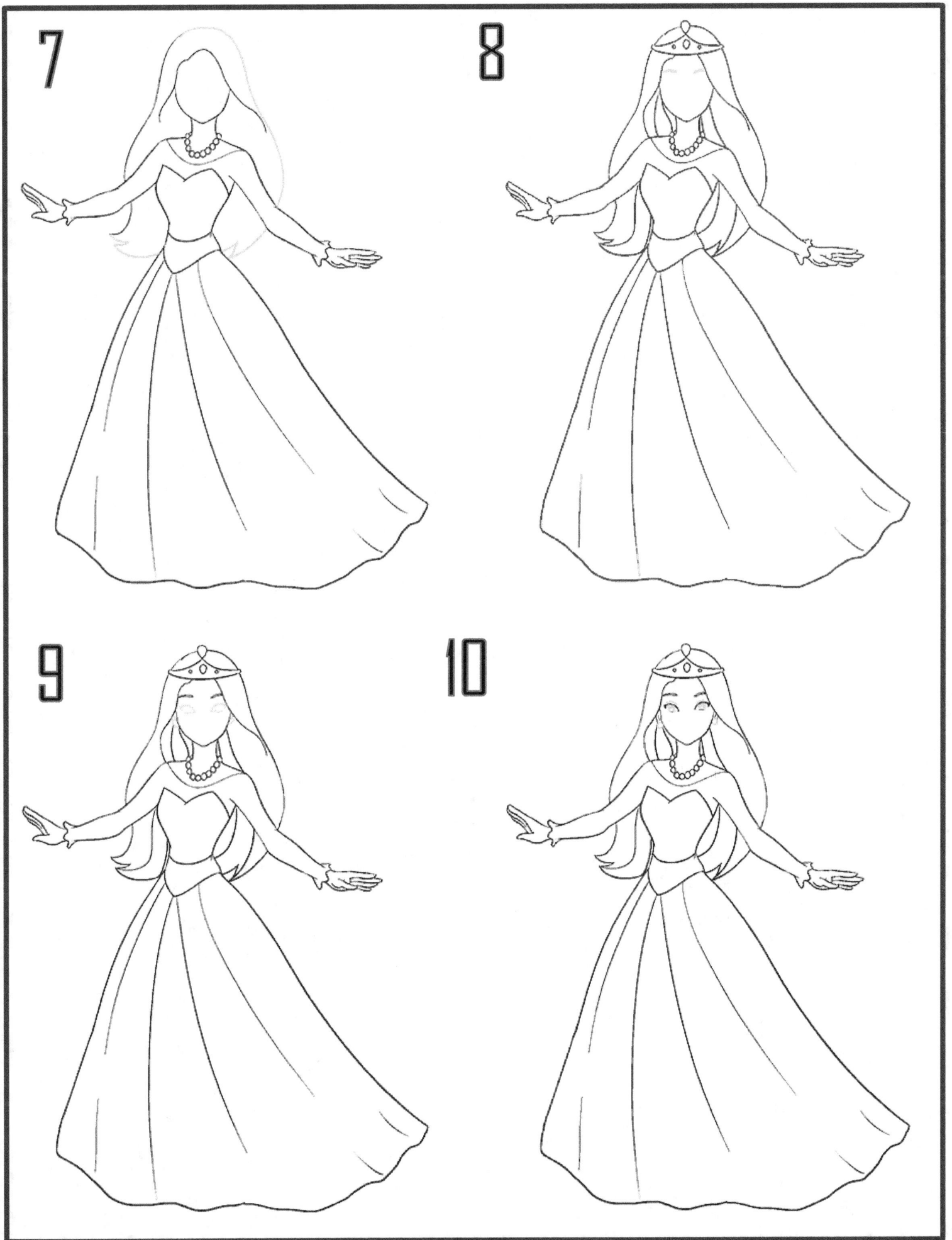

1

2

3

4

5

6

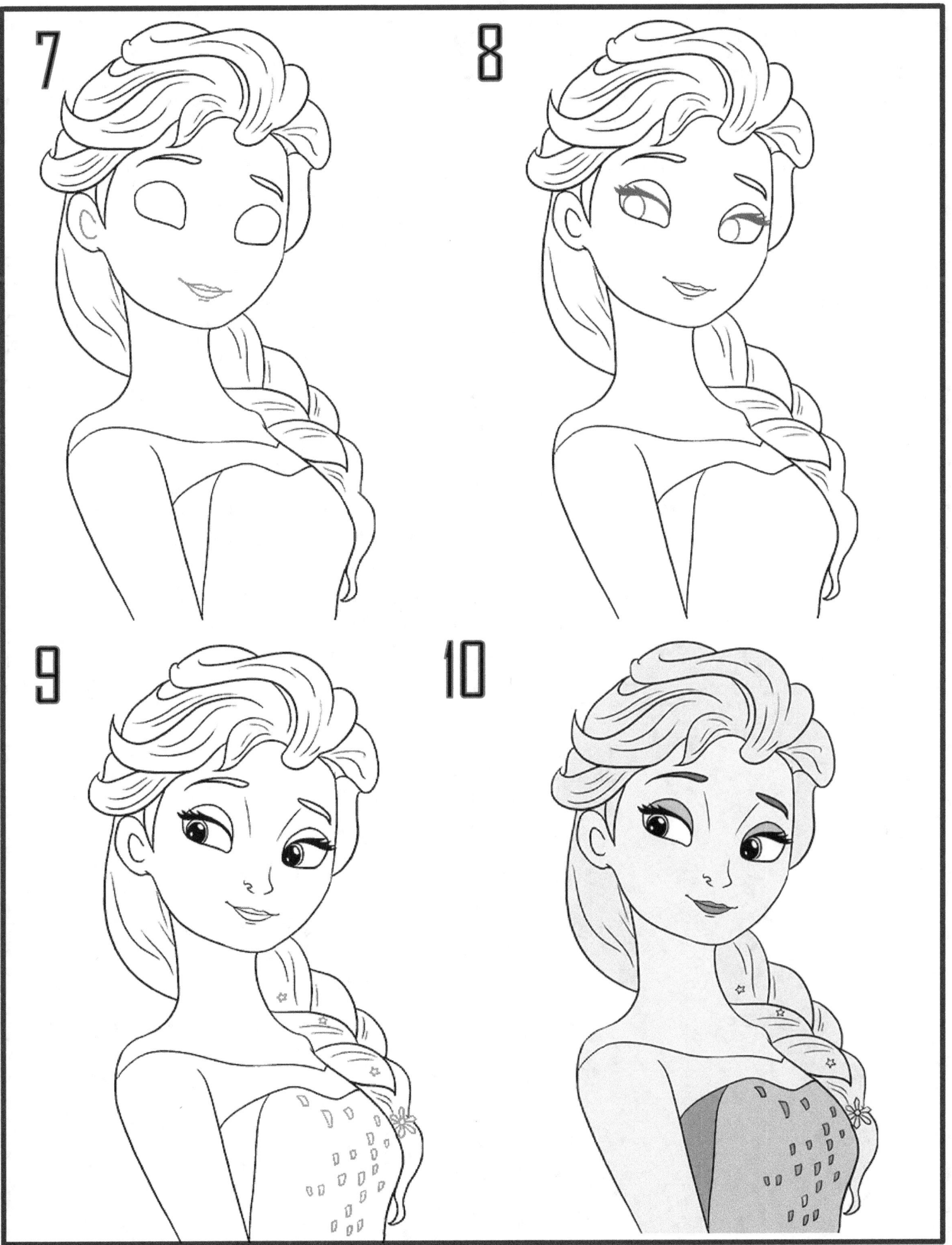

1

2

3

4

5

6

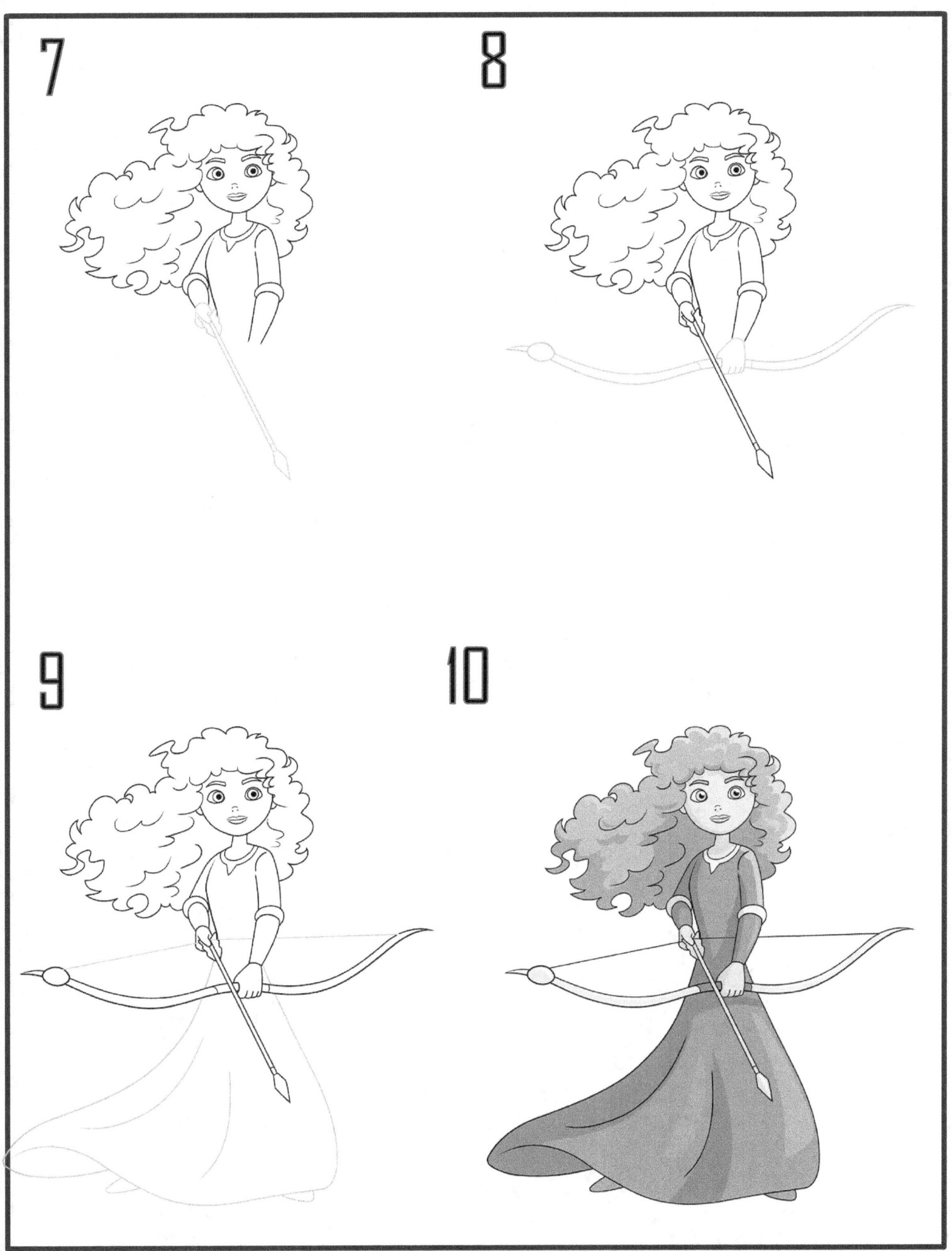

1

2

3

4

5

6

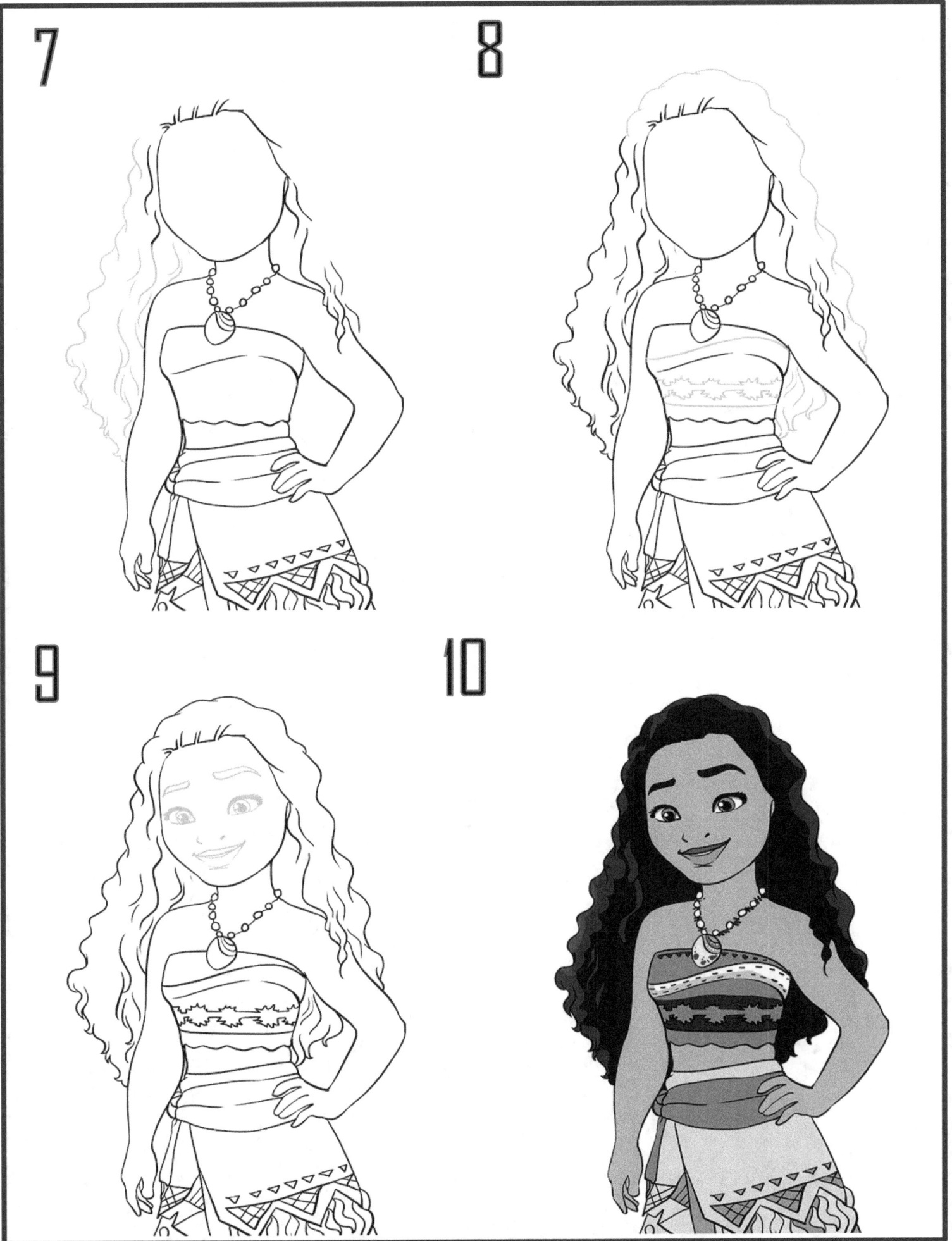

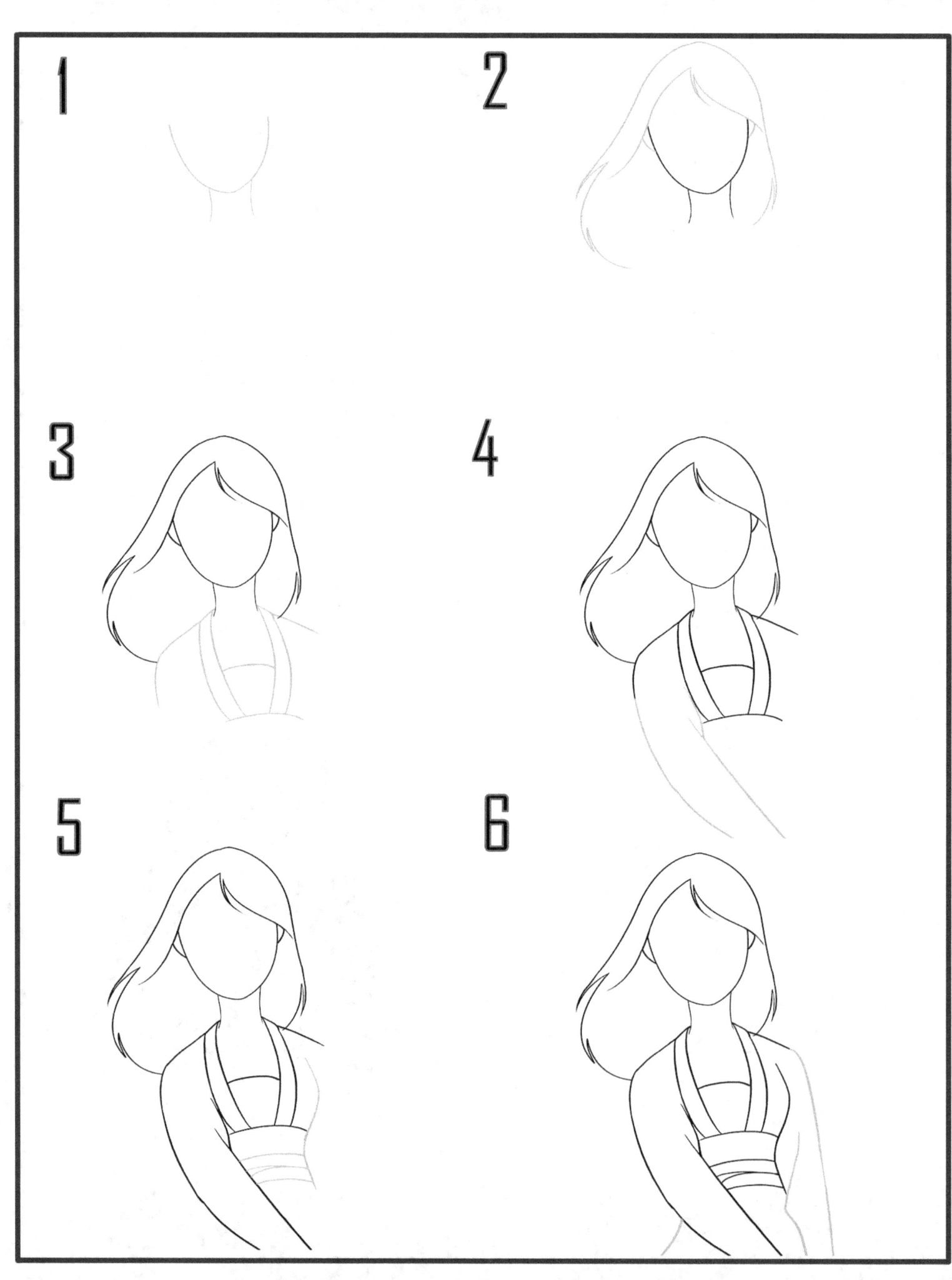

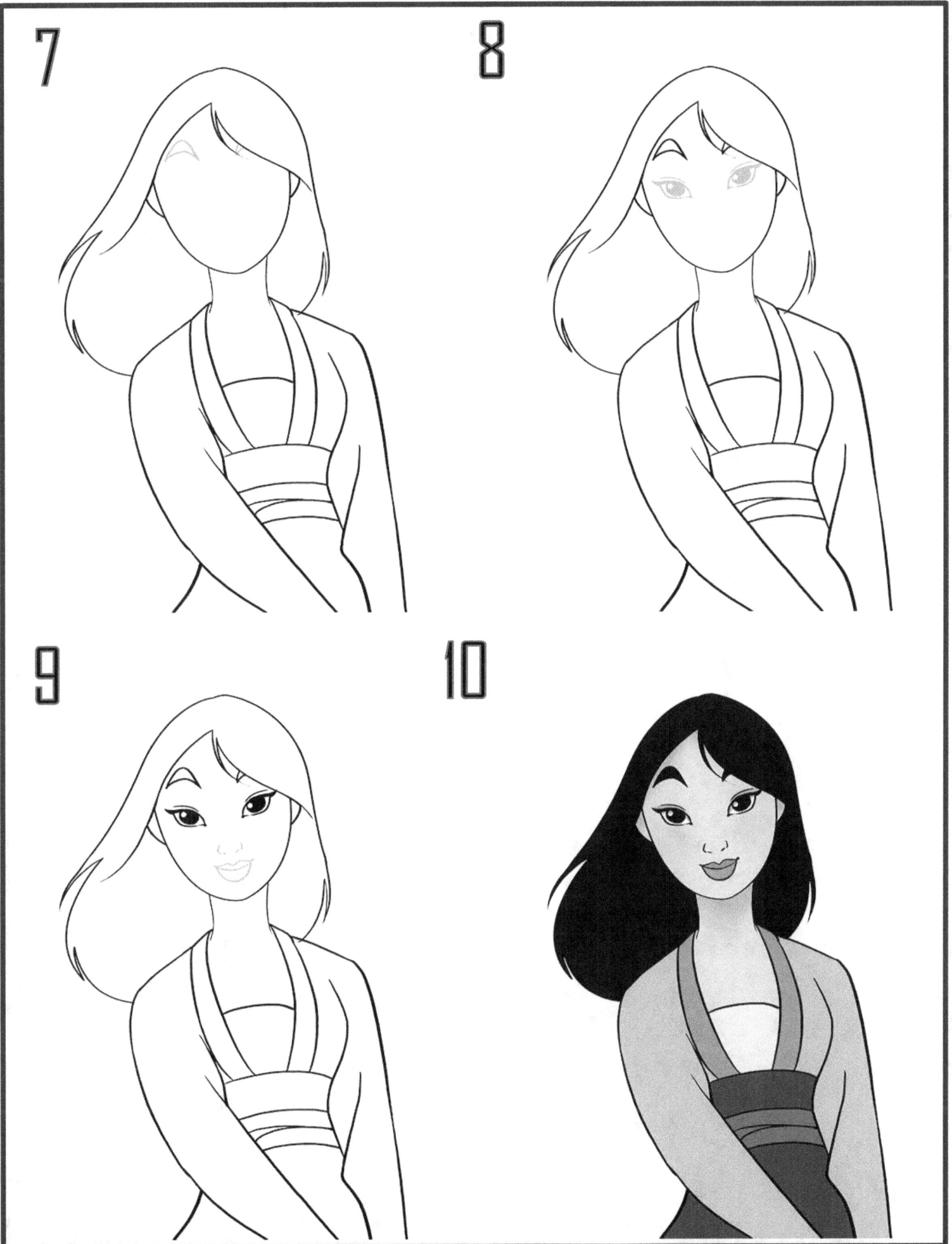

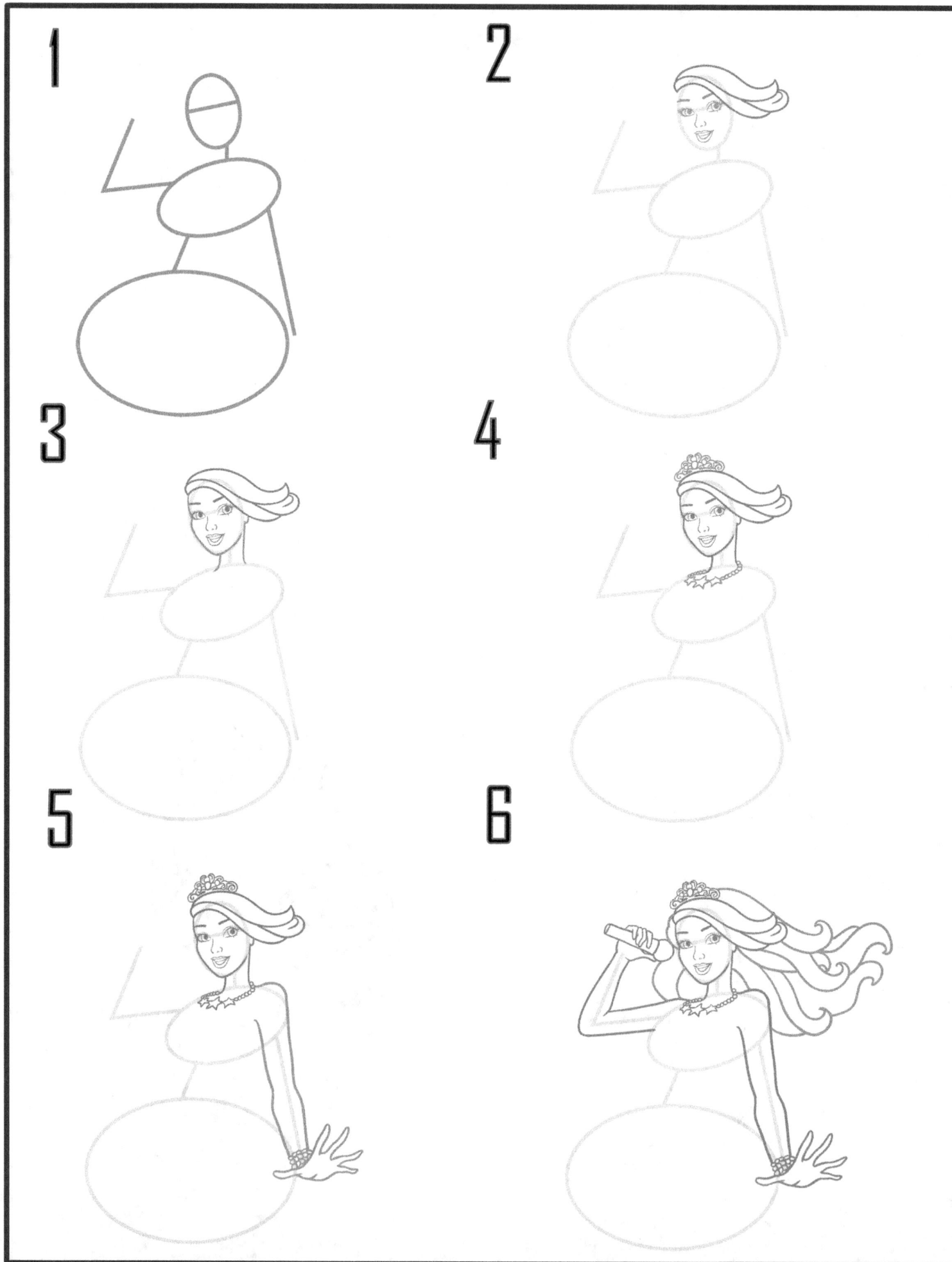

7

8

9

10

Part 2 how to draw a unicorn

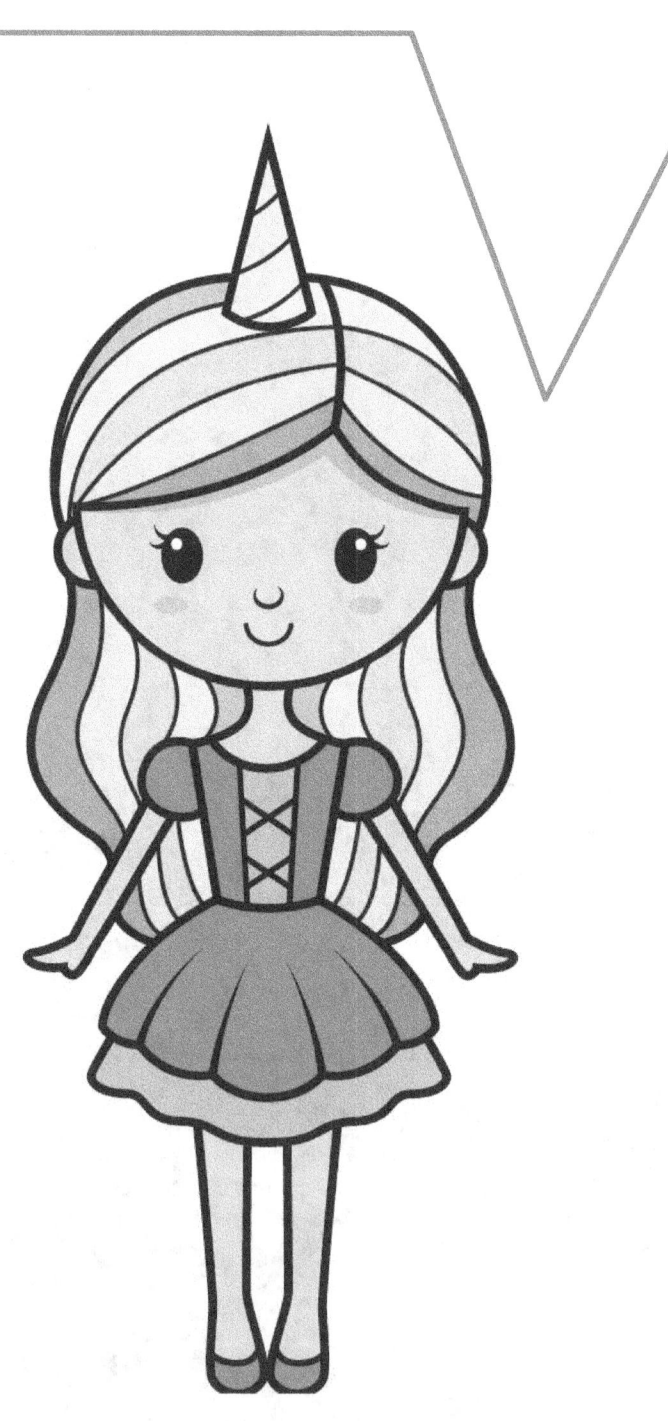

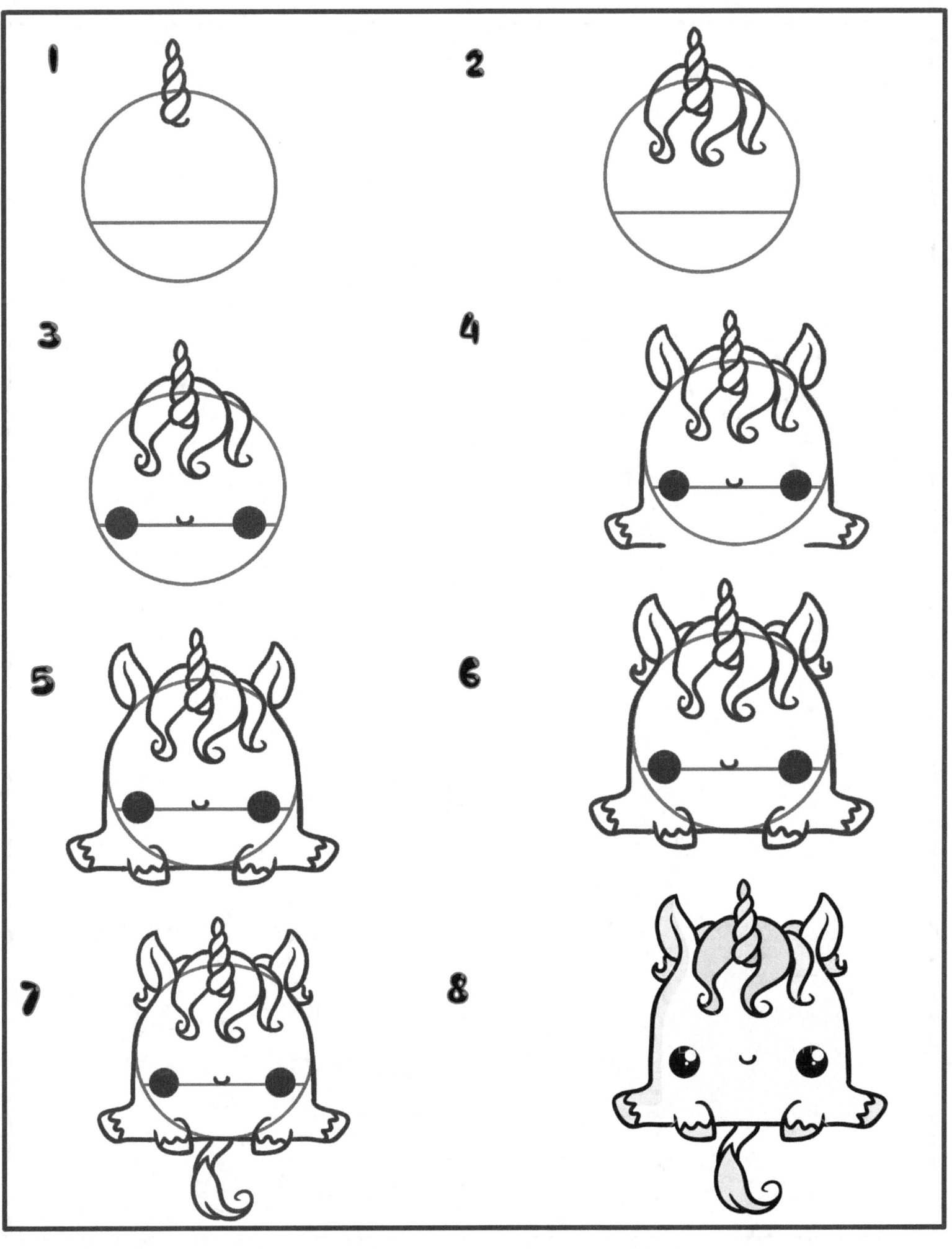

1

2

3

4

5

6

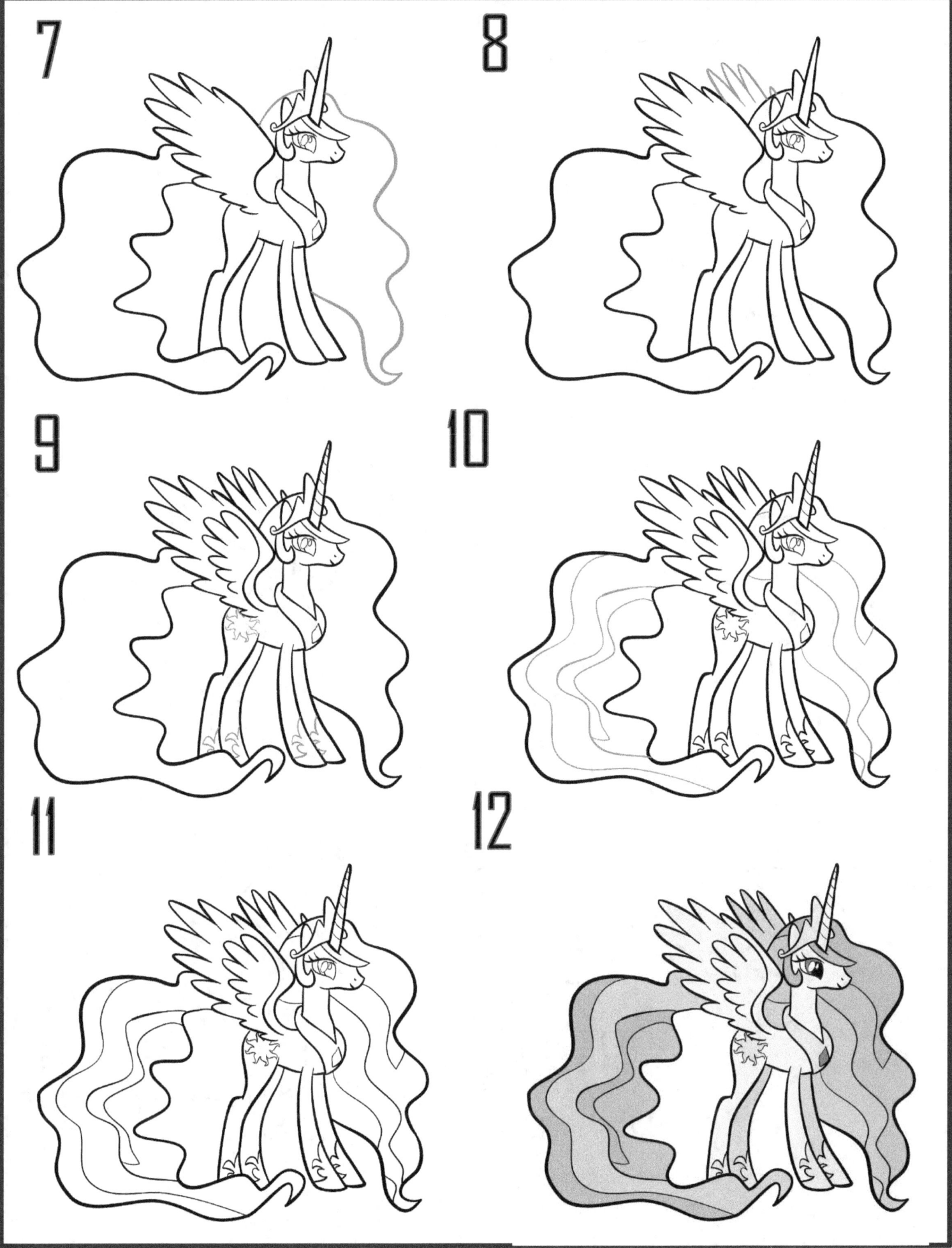

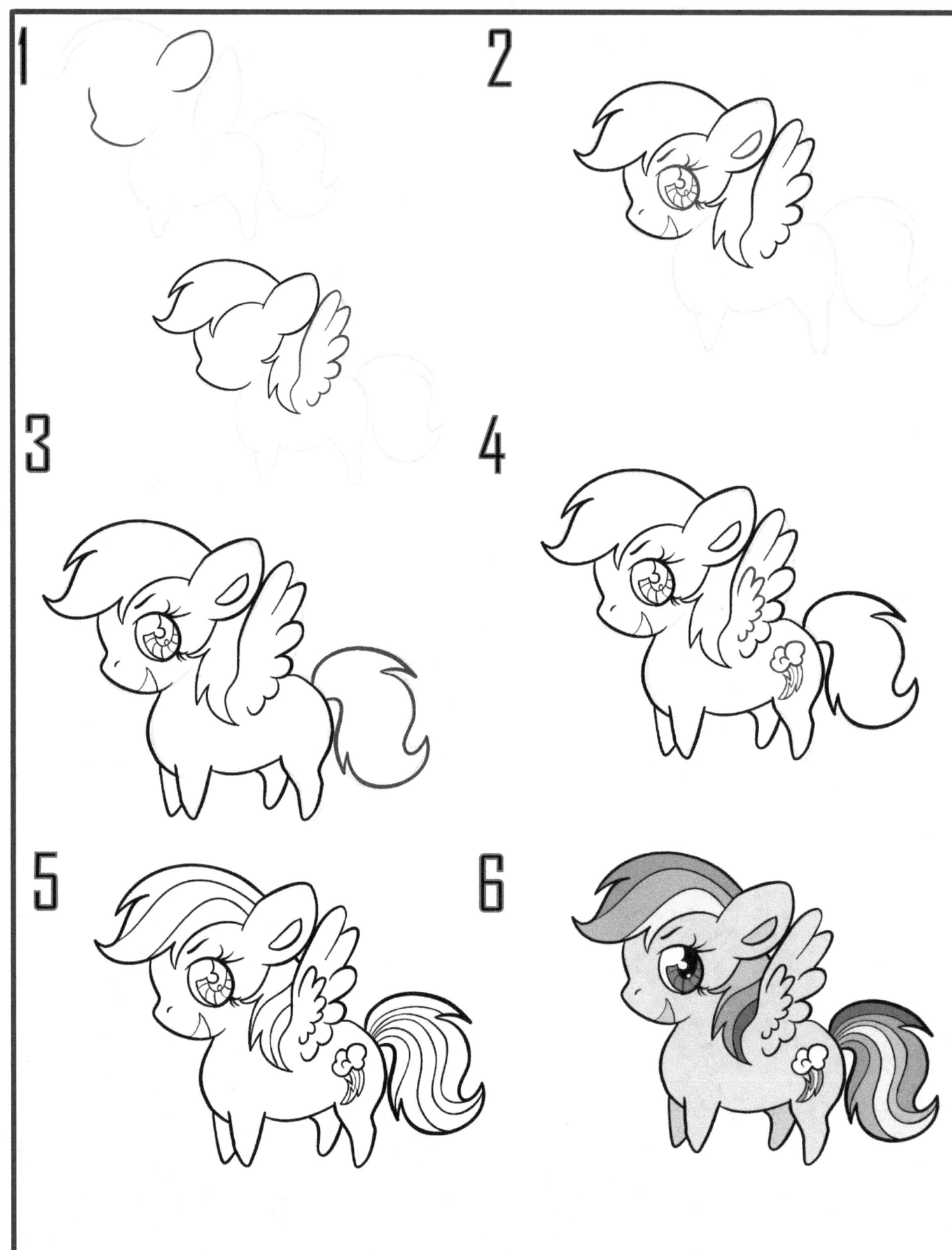

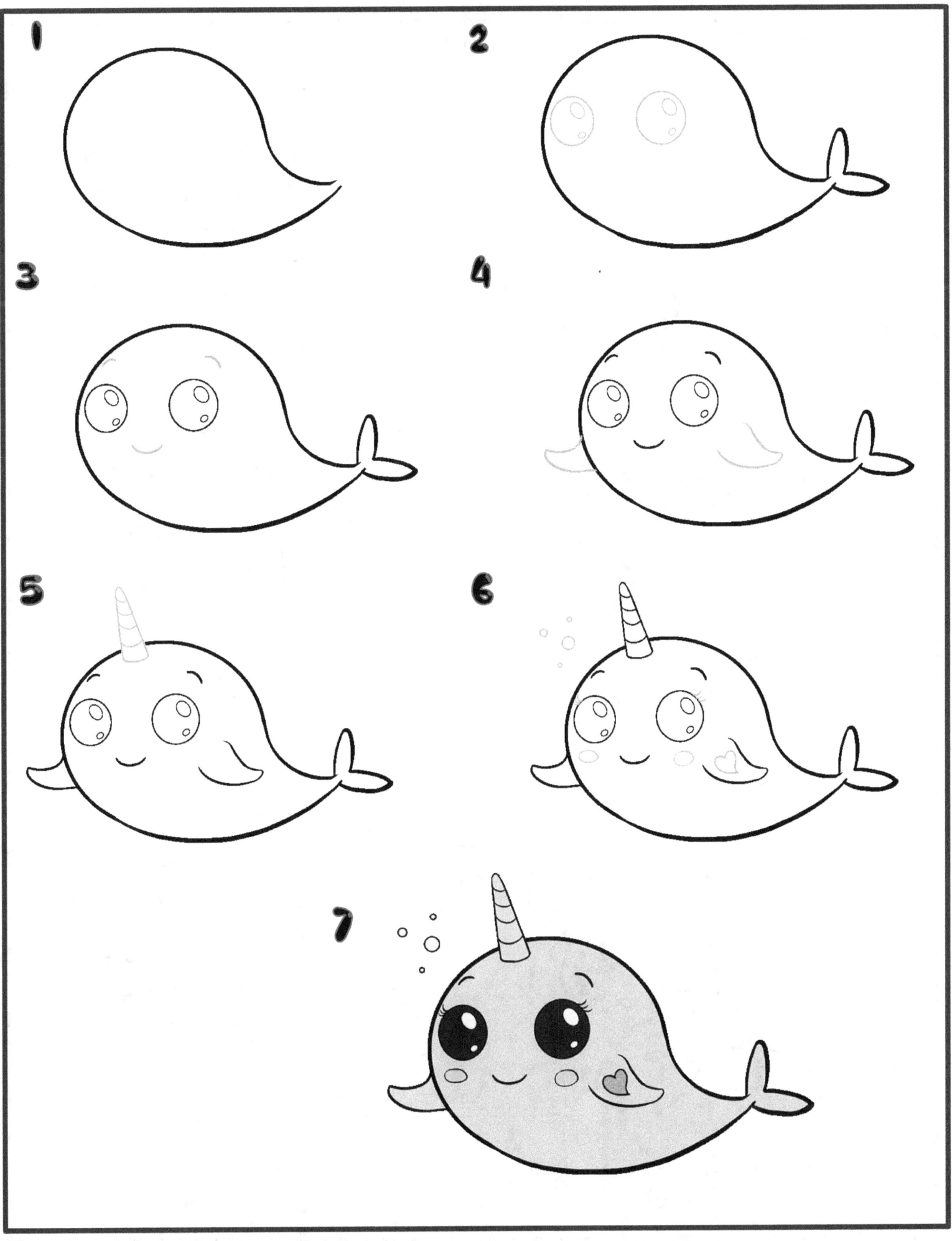

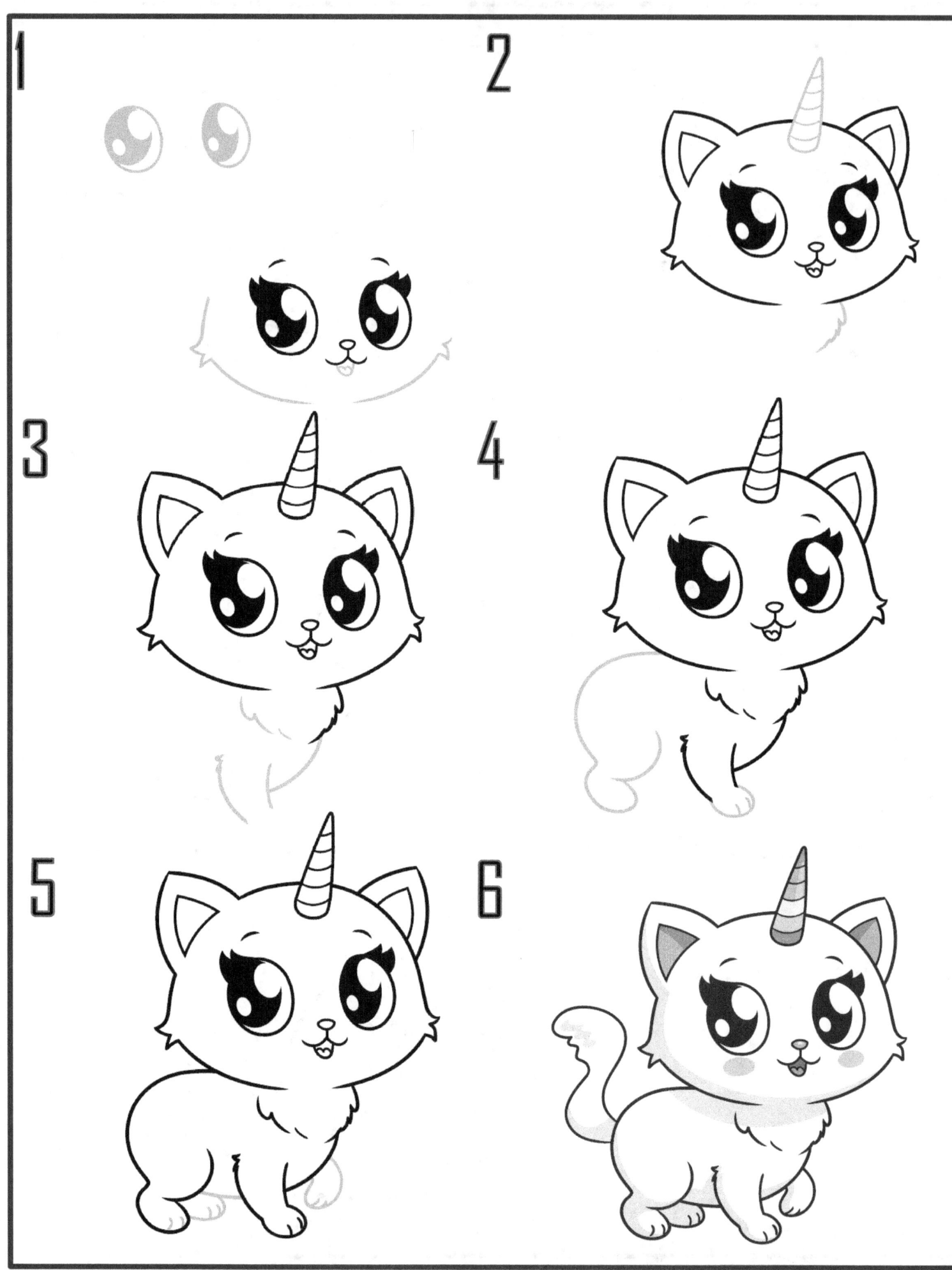

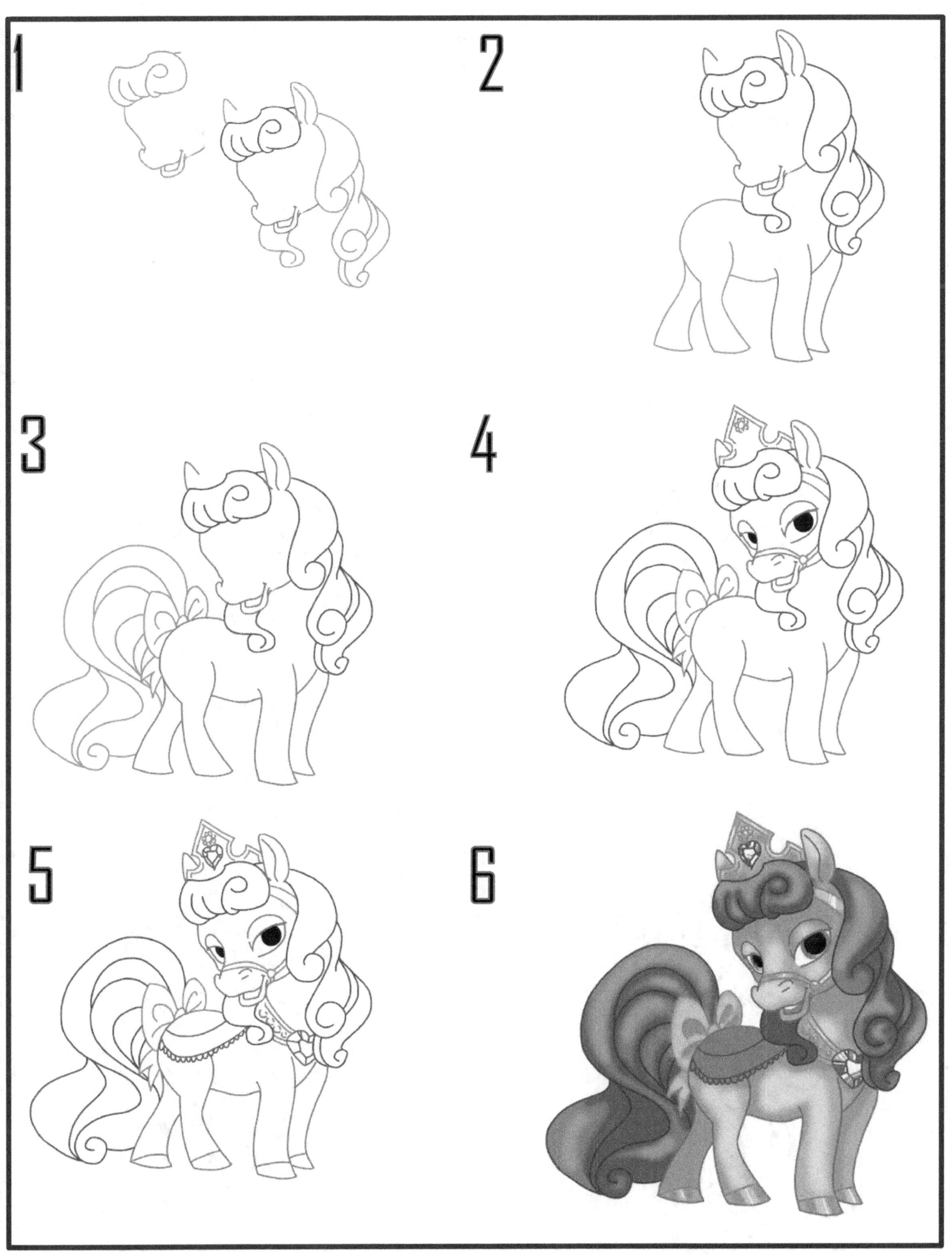

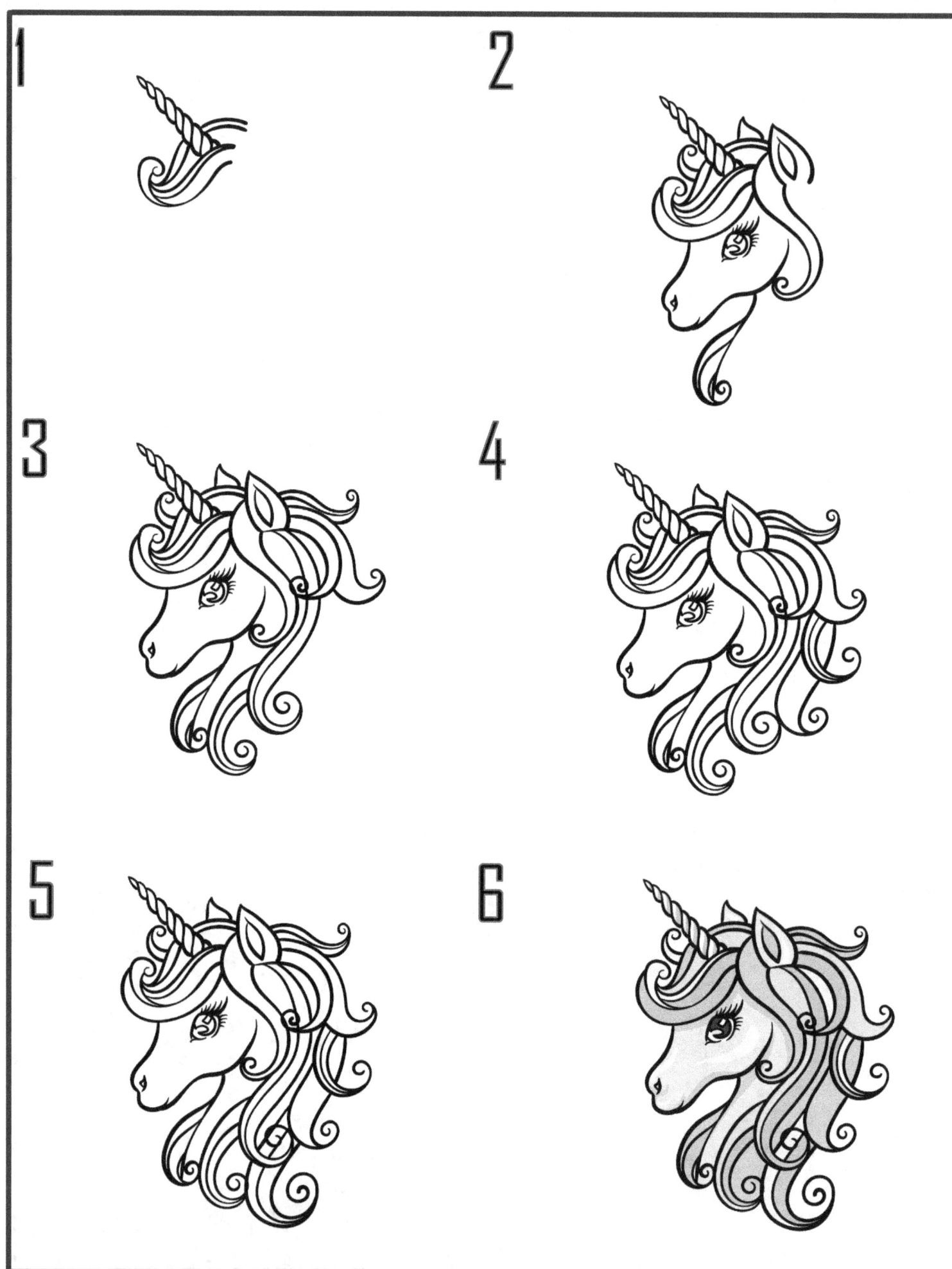

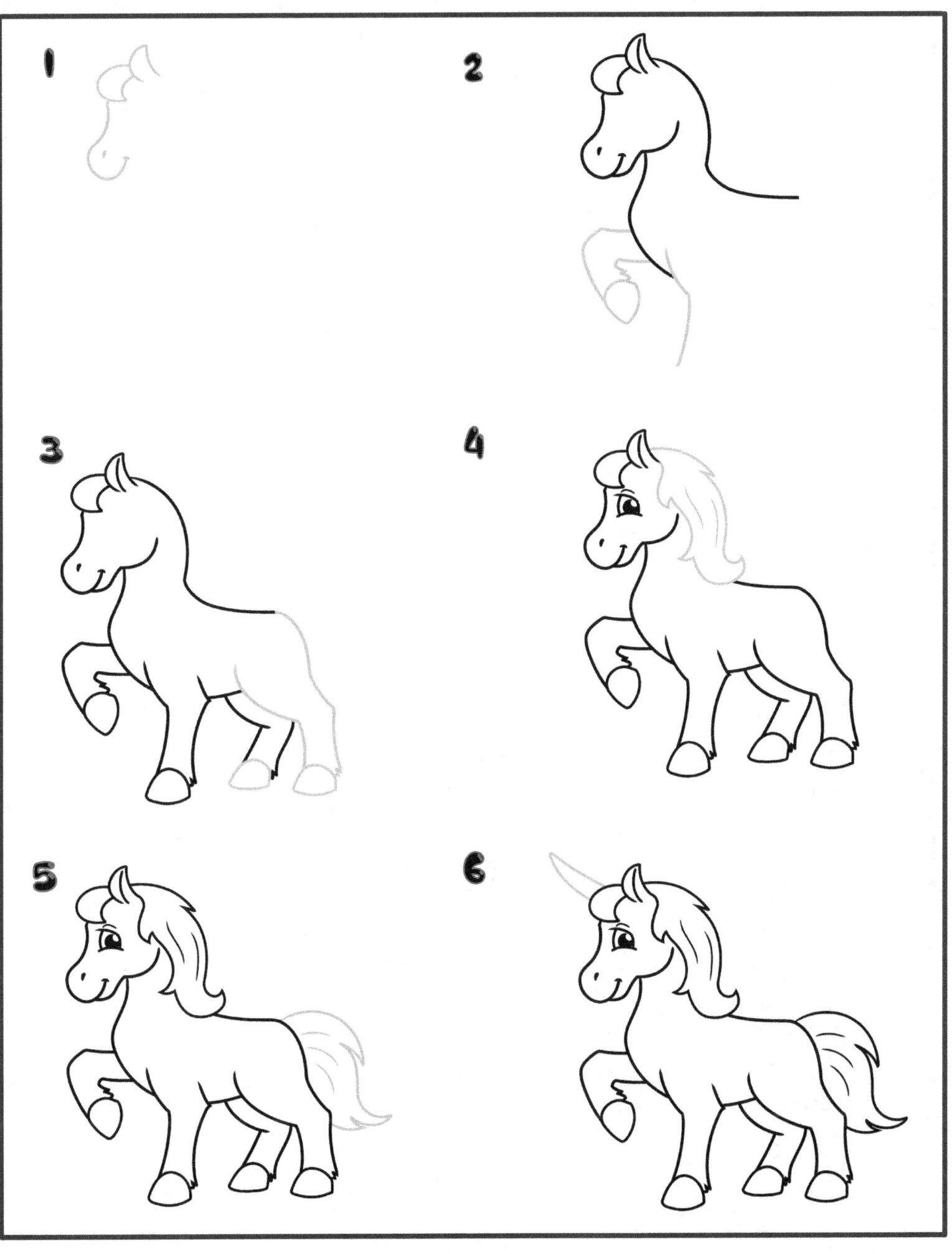

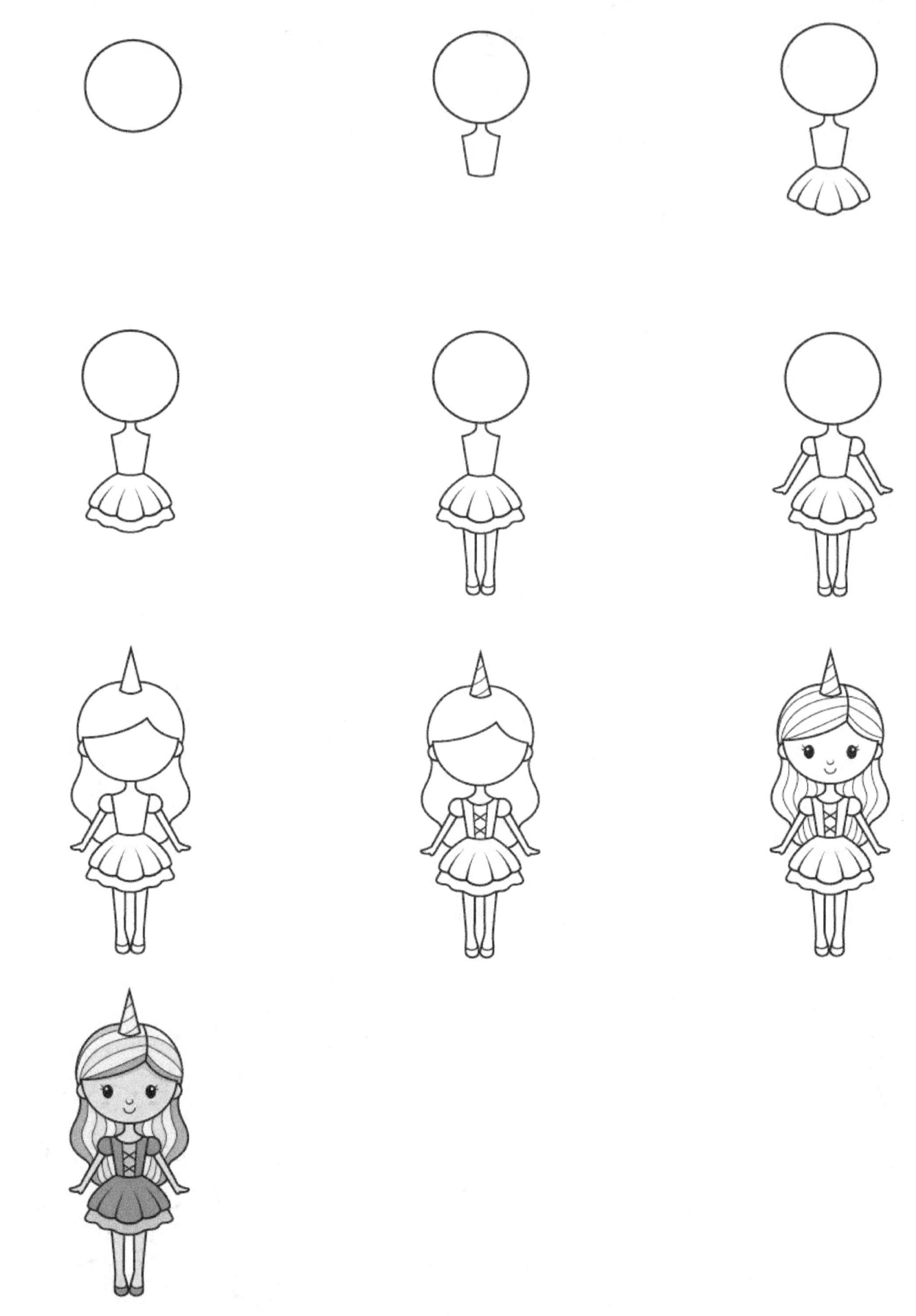

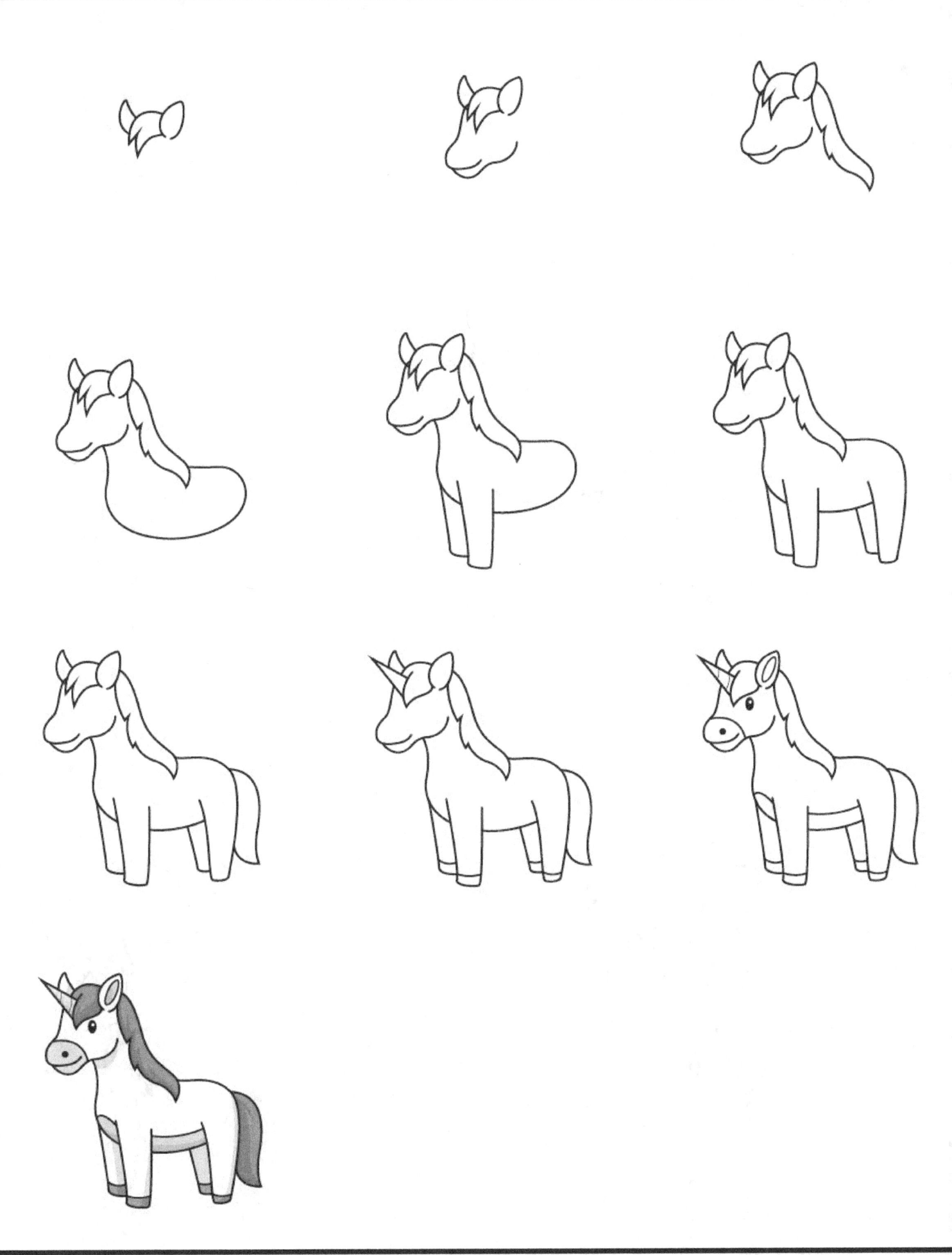

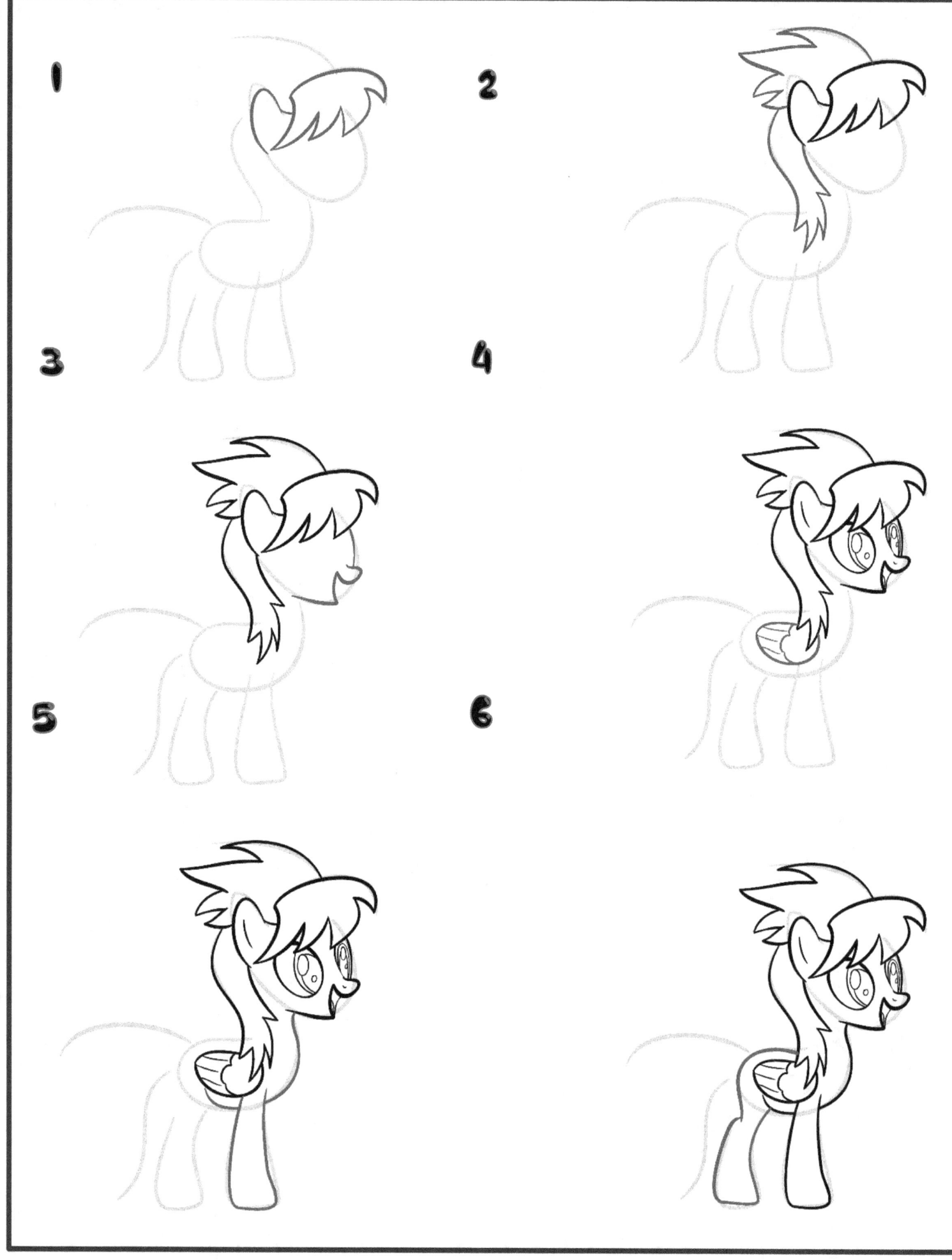

7

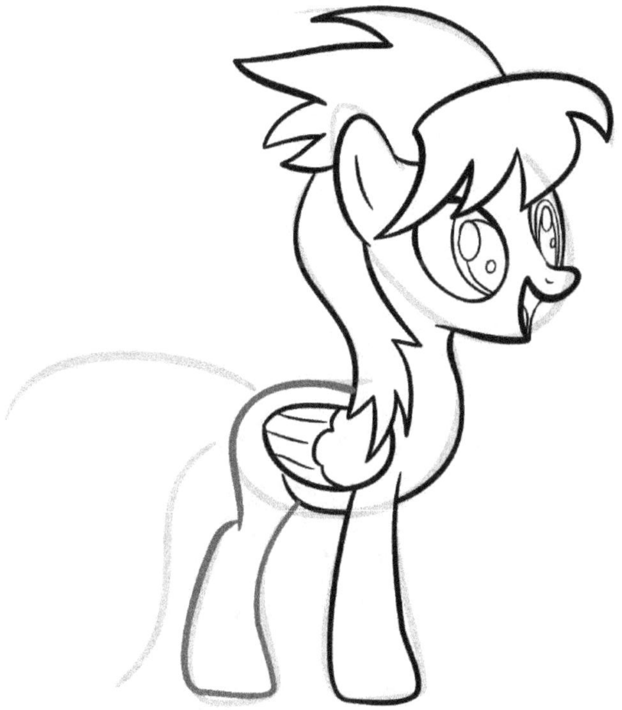

8

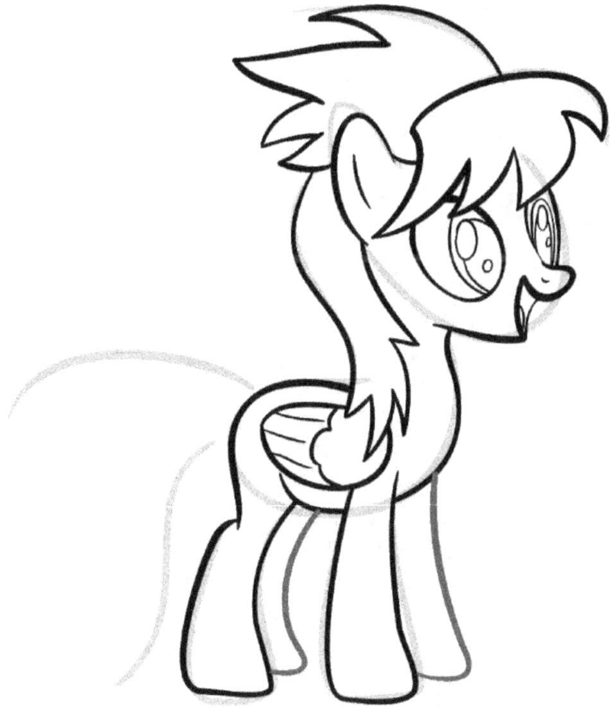

9

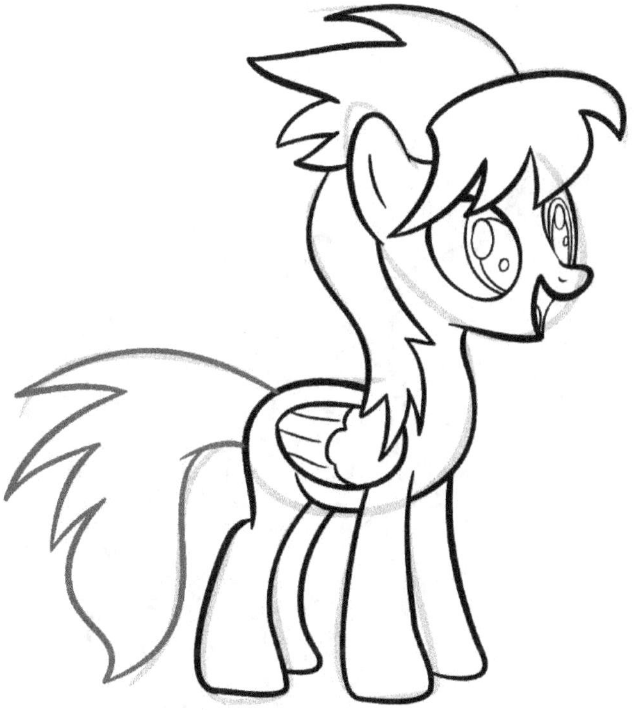

10

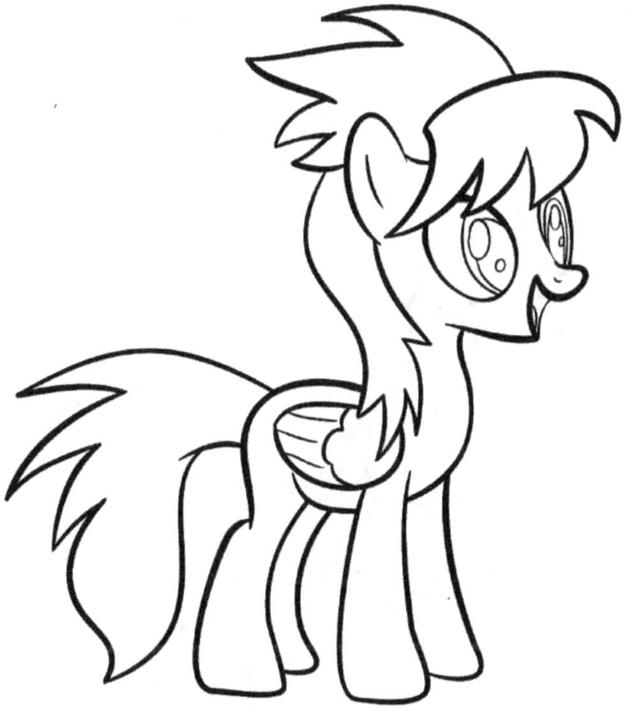

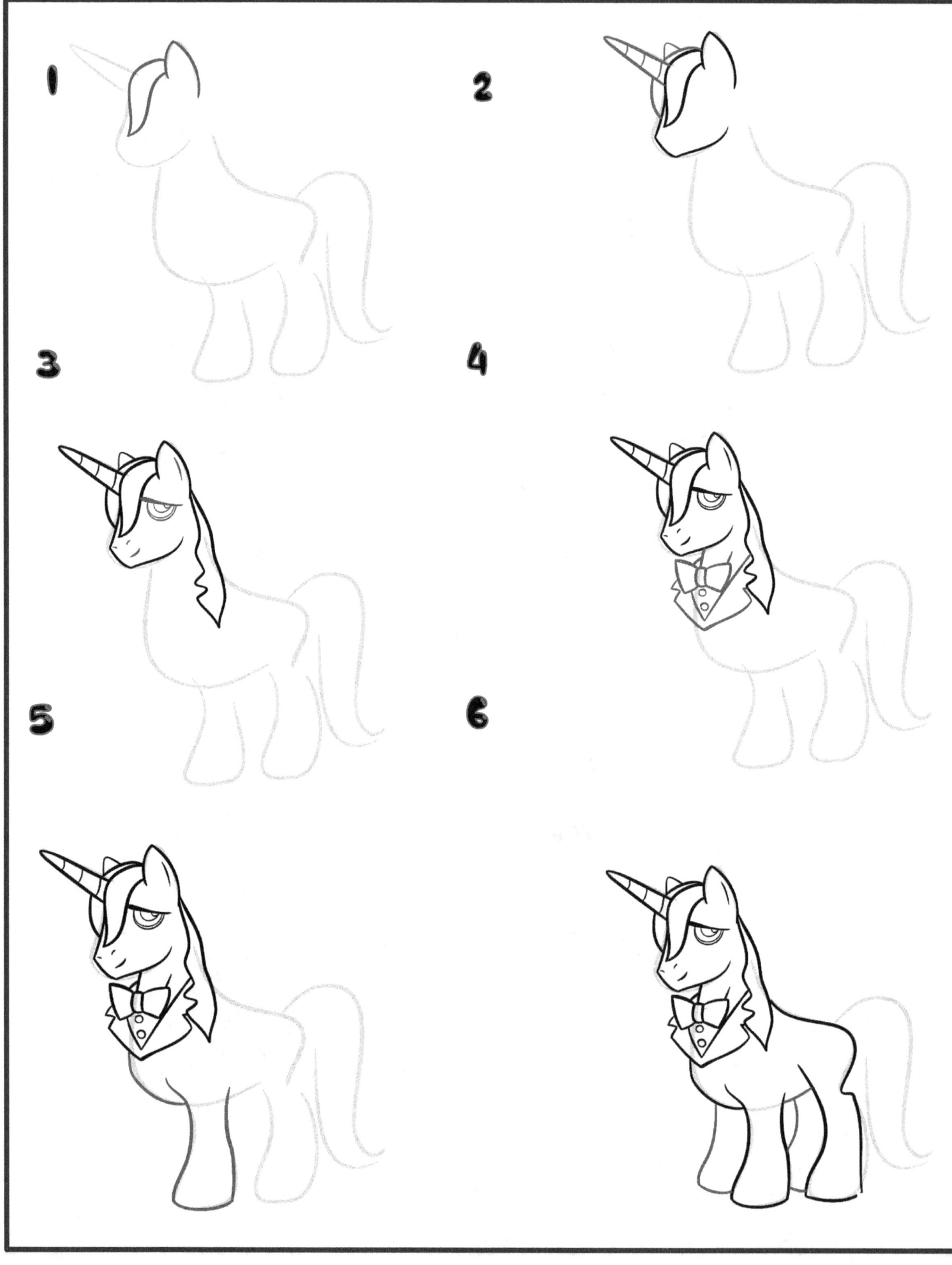

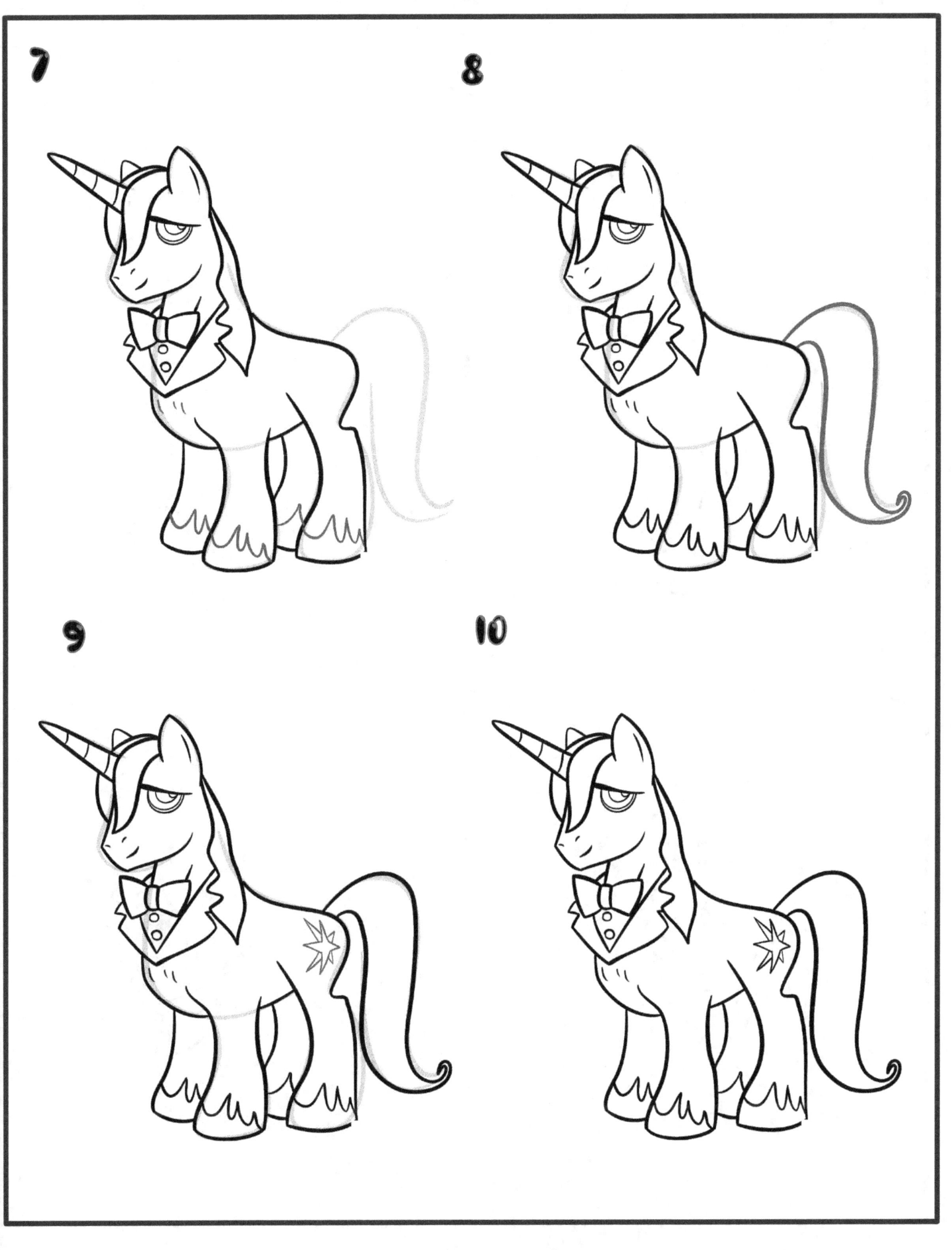

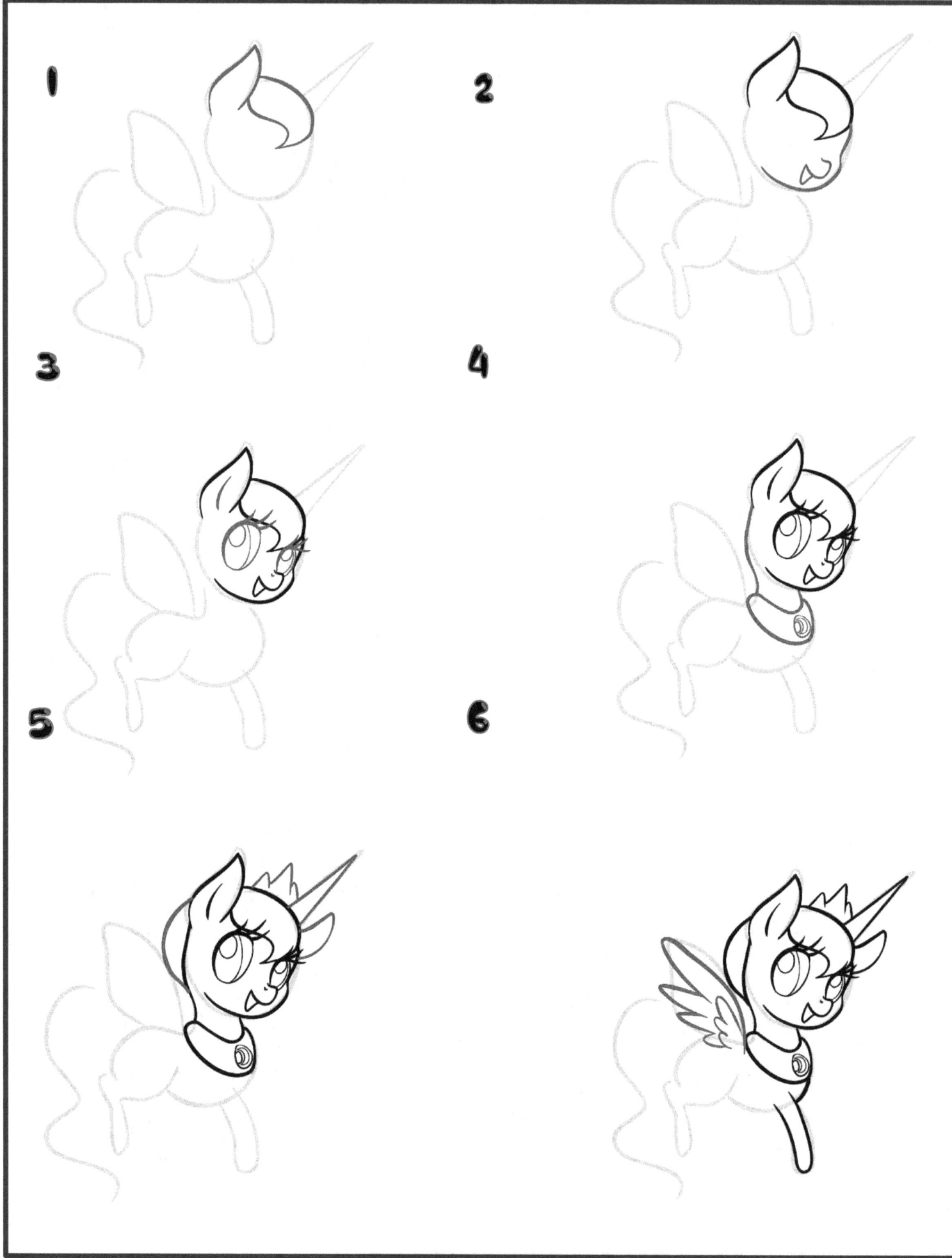

7

8

9

10

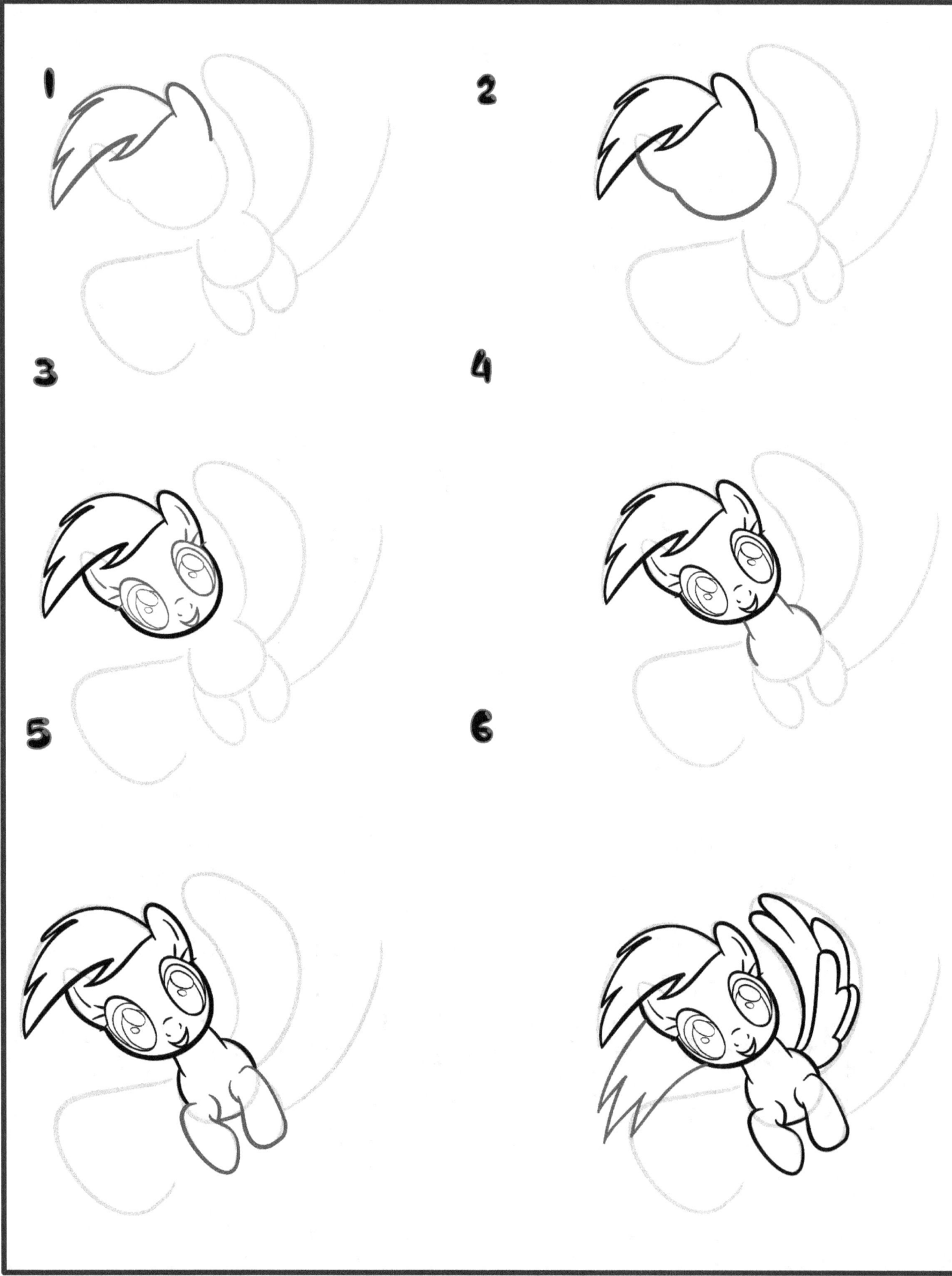

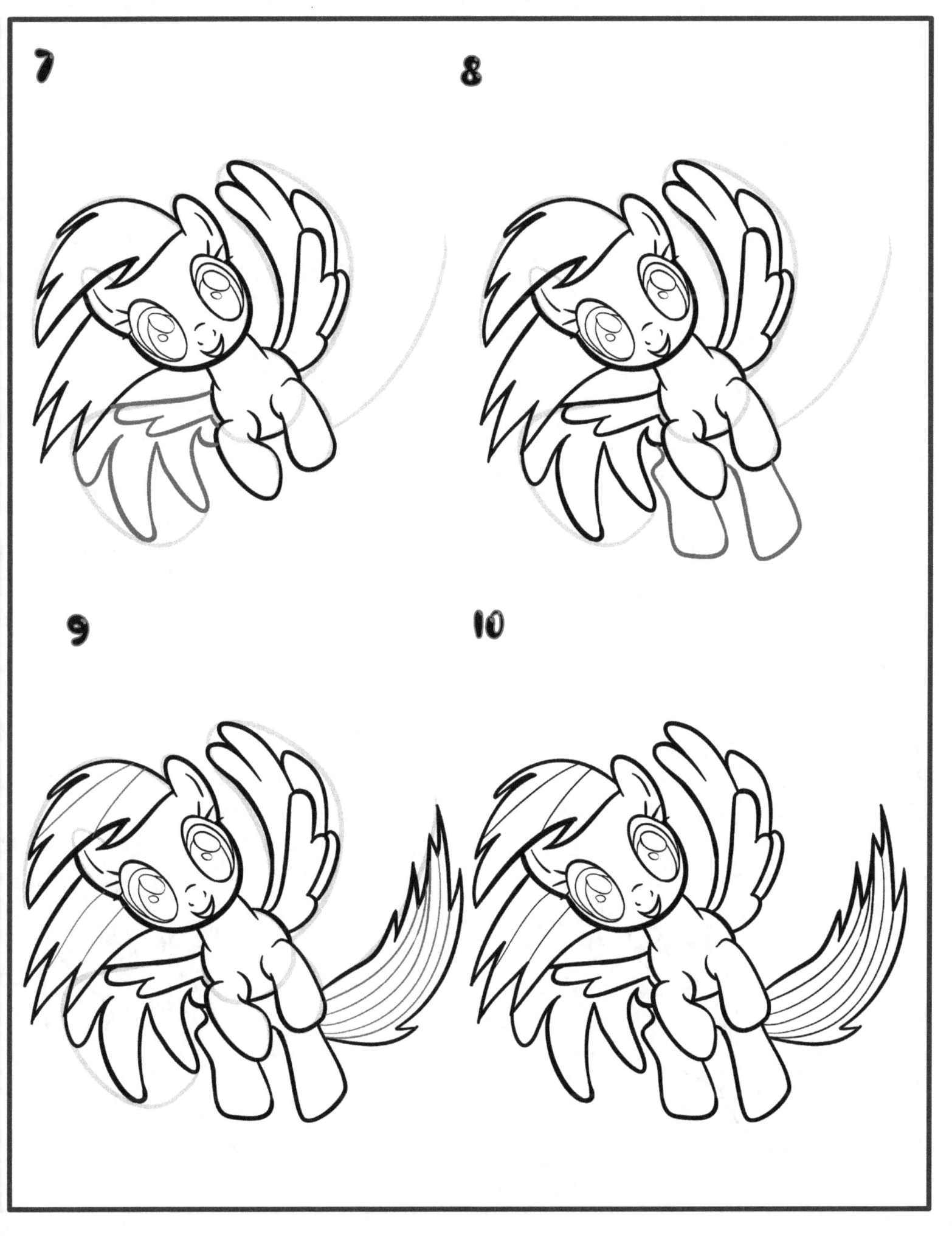

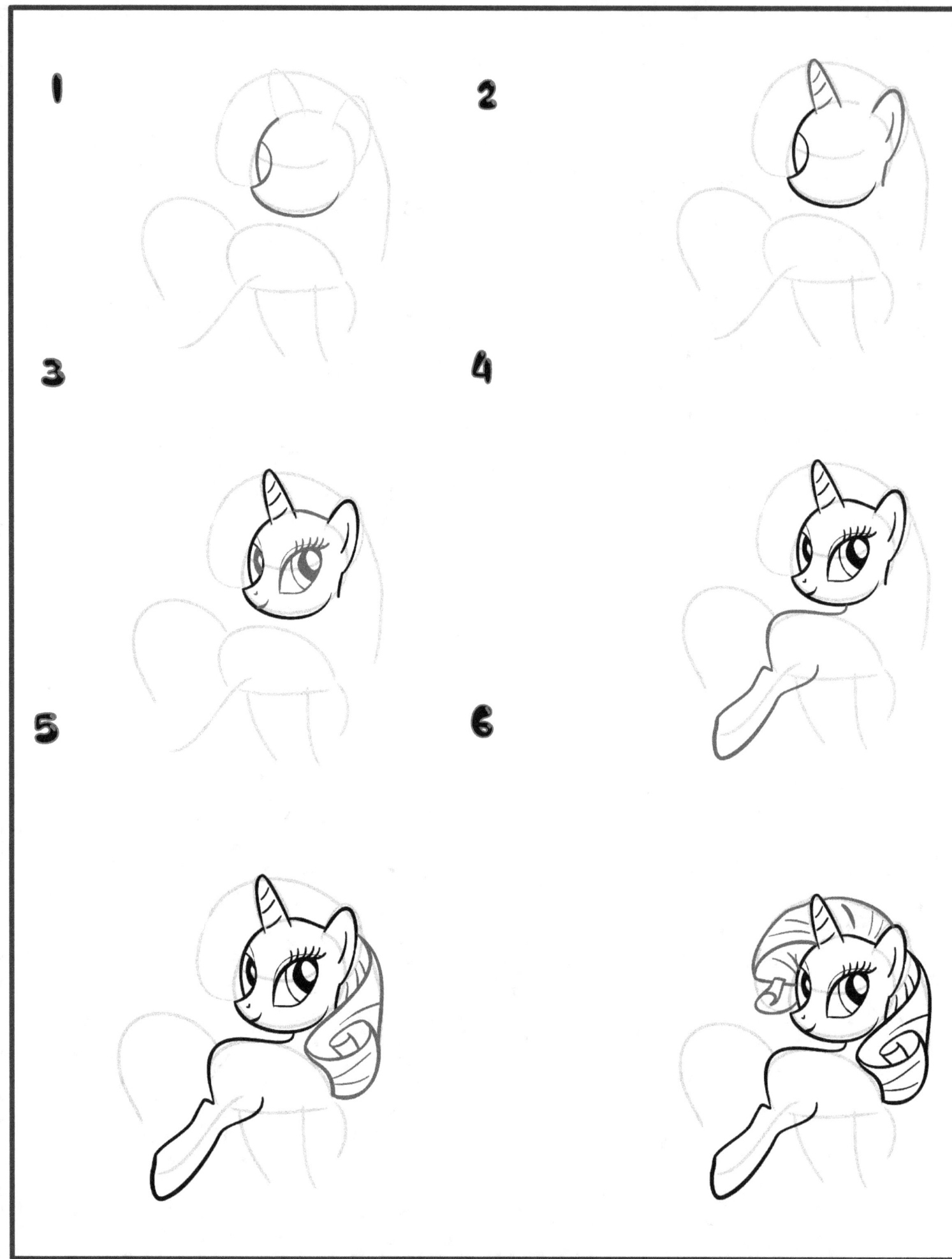

7

8

9

10

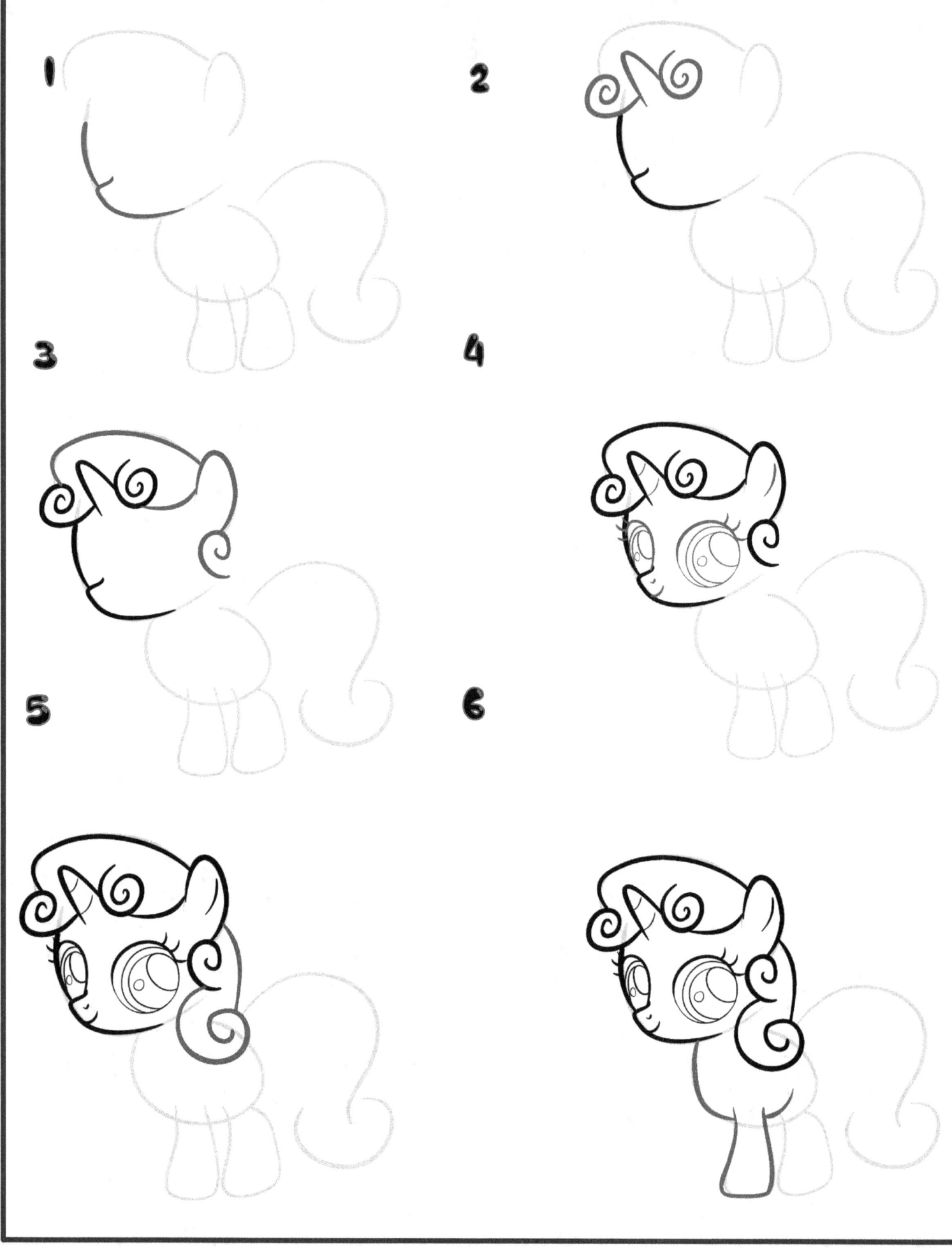

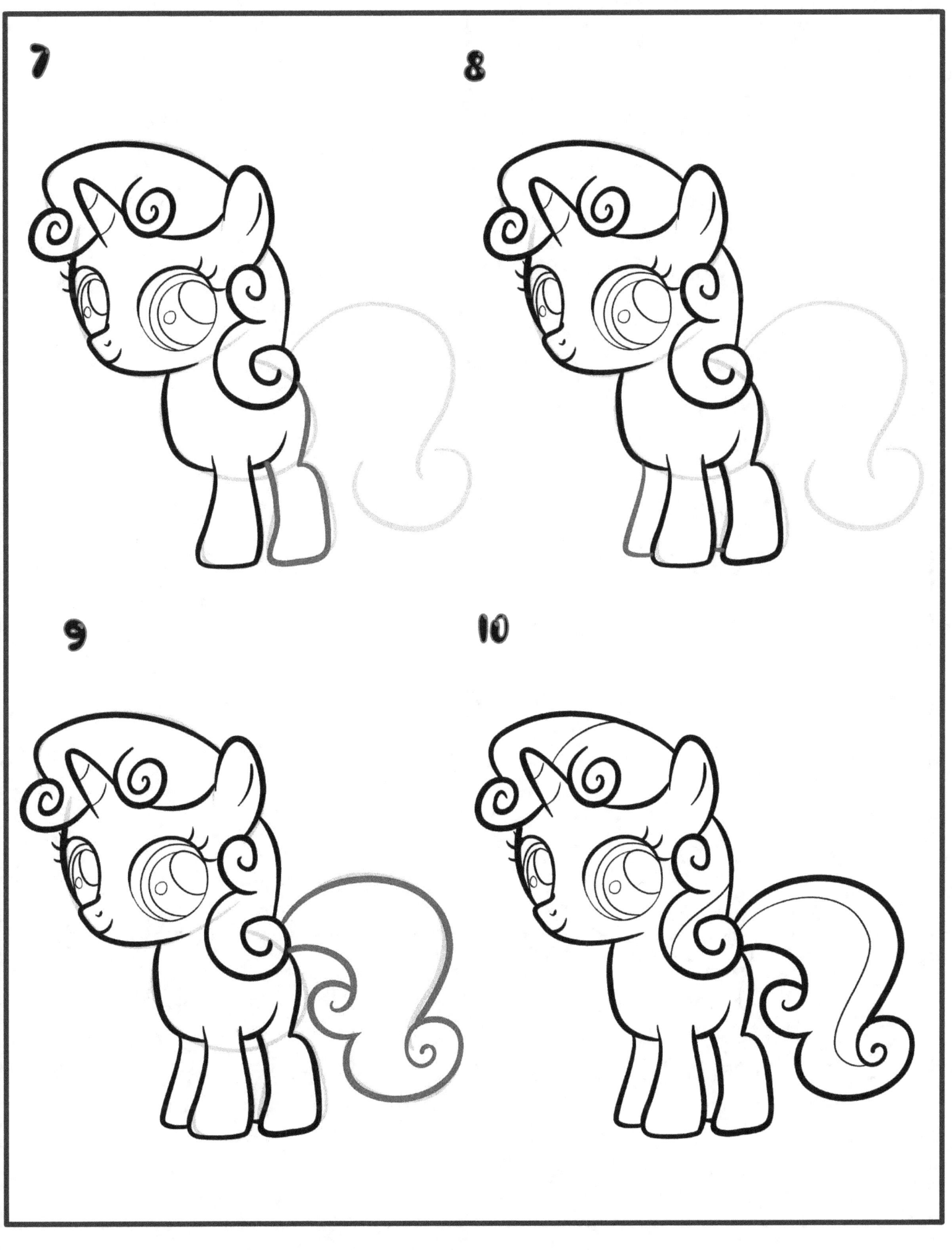

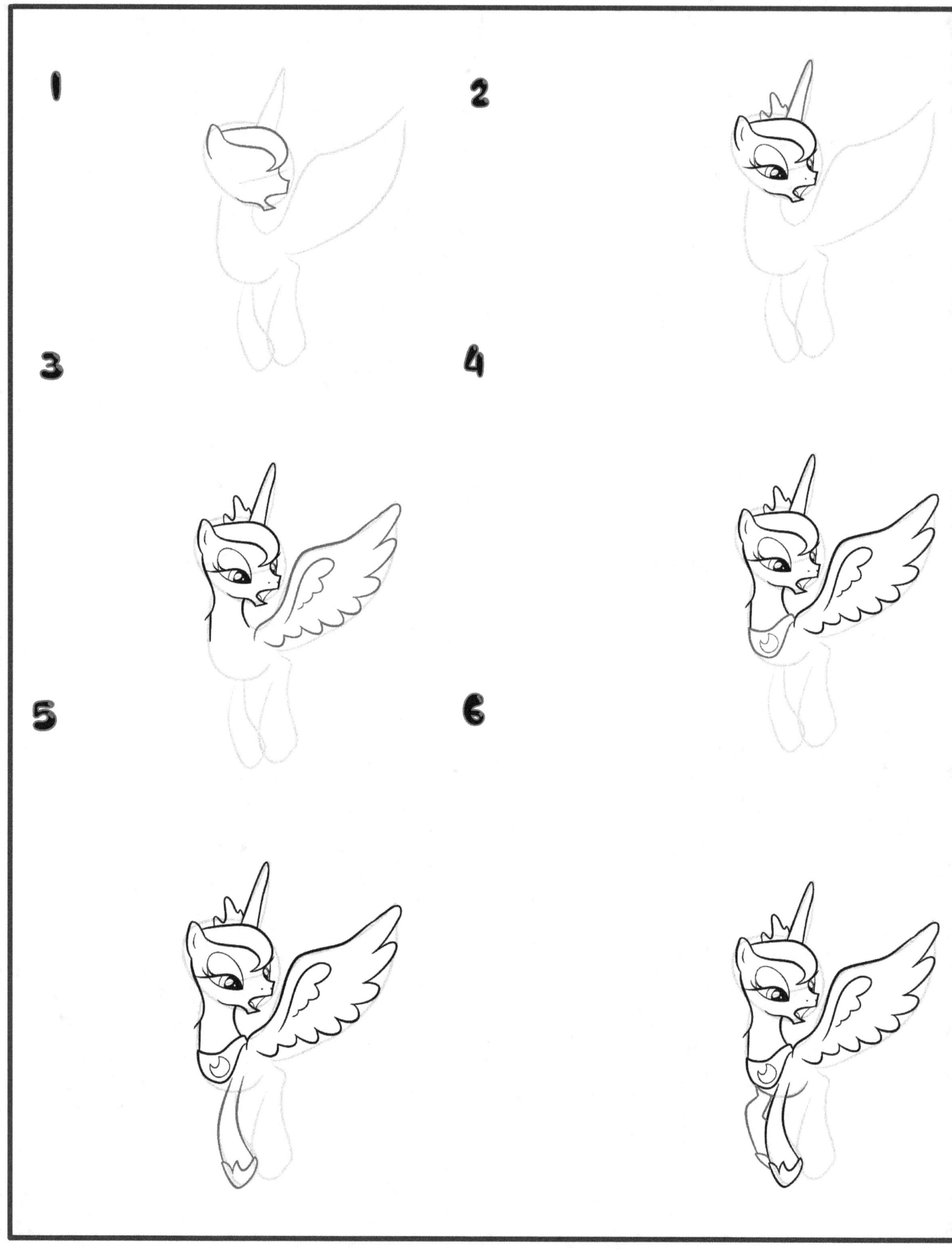

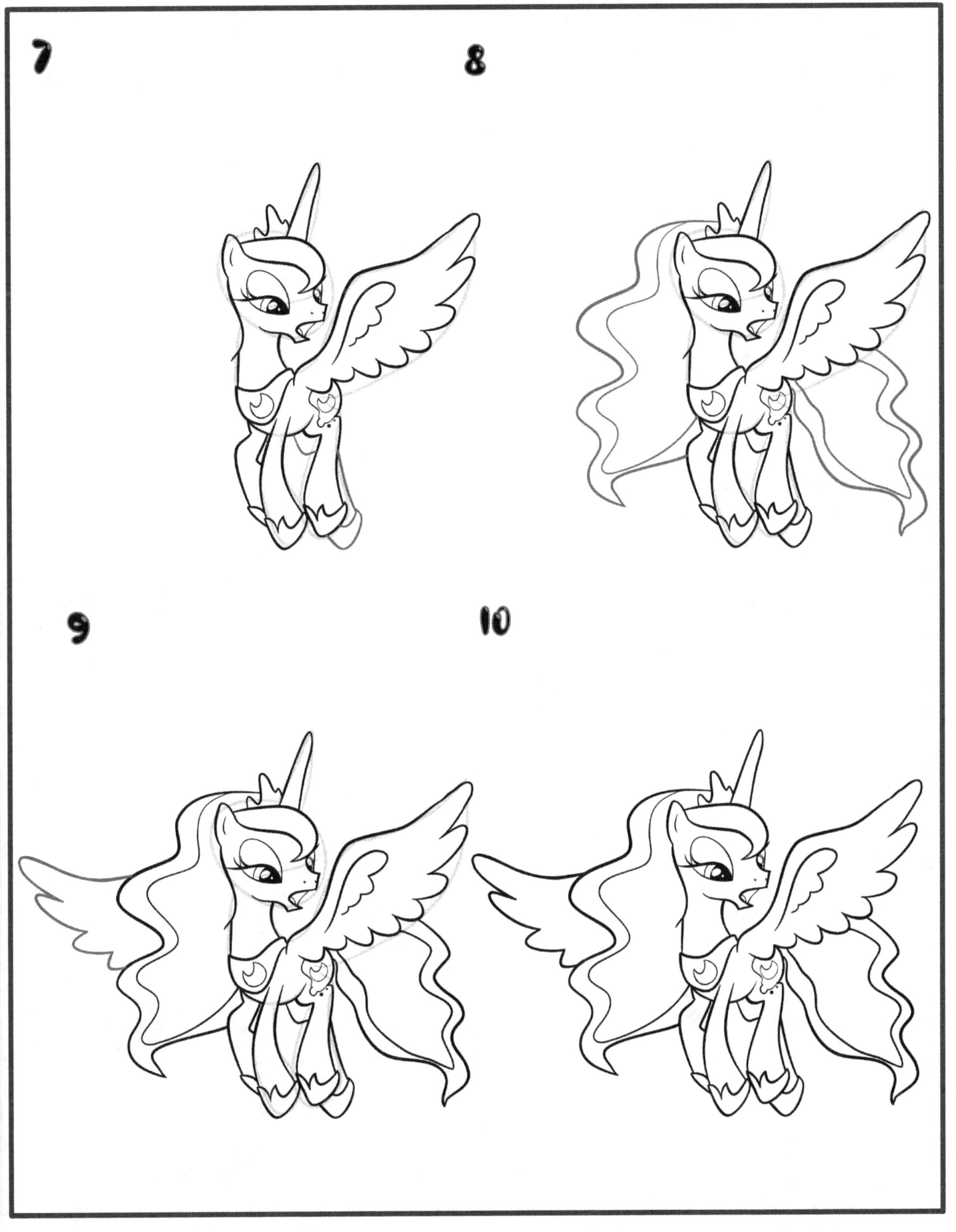

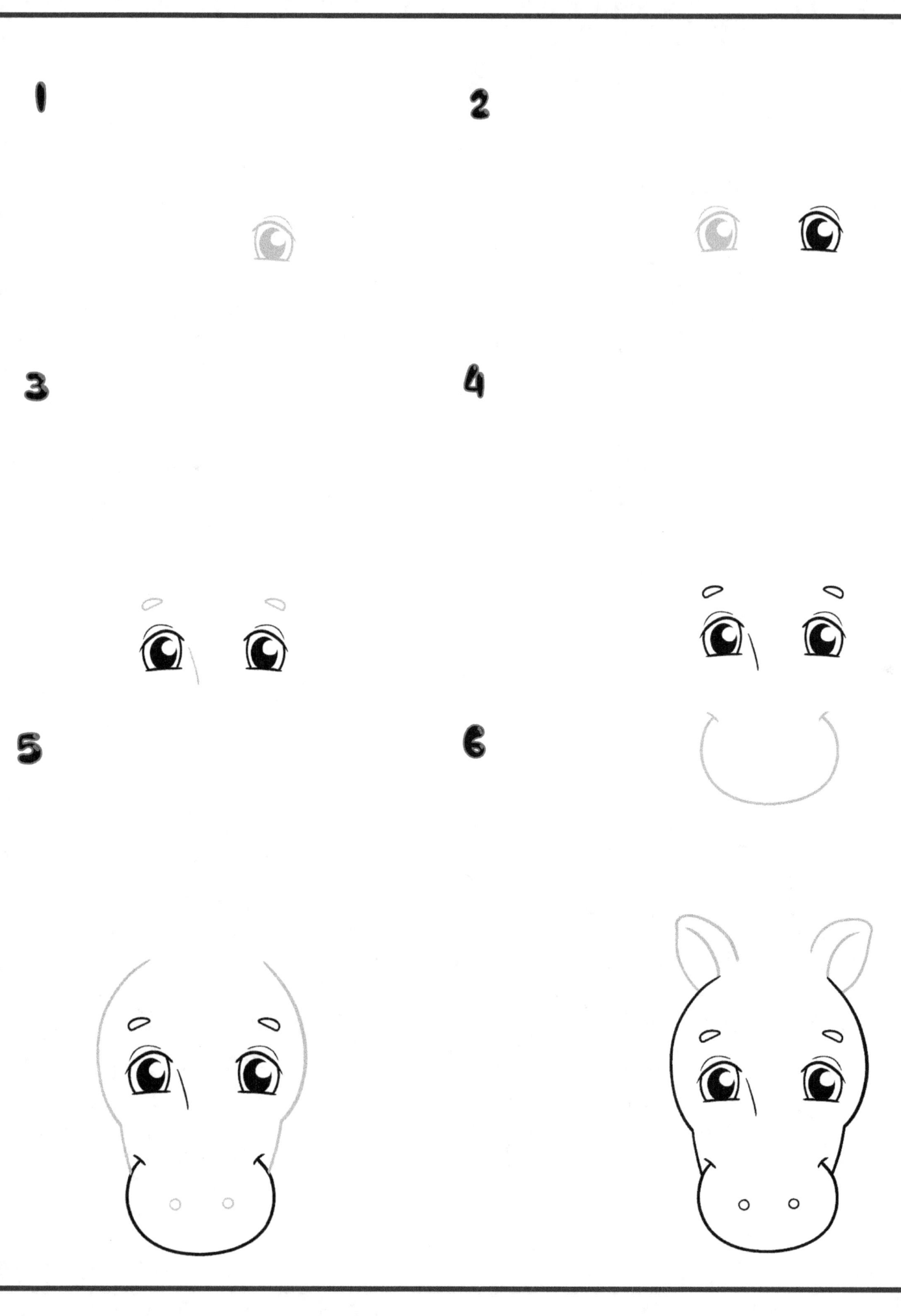

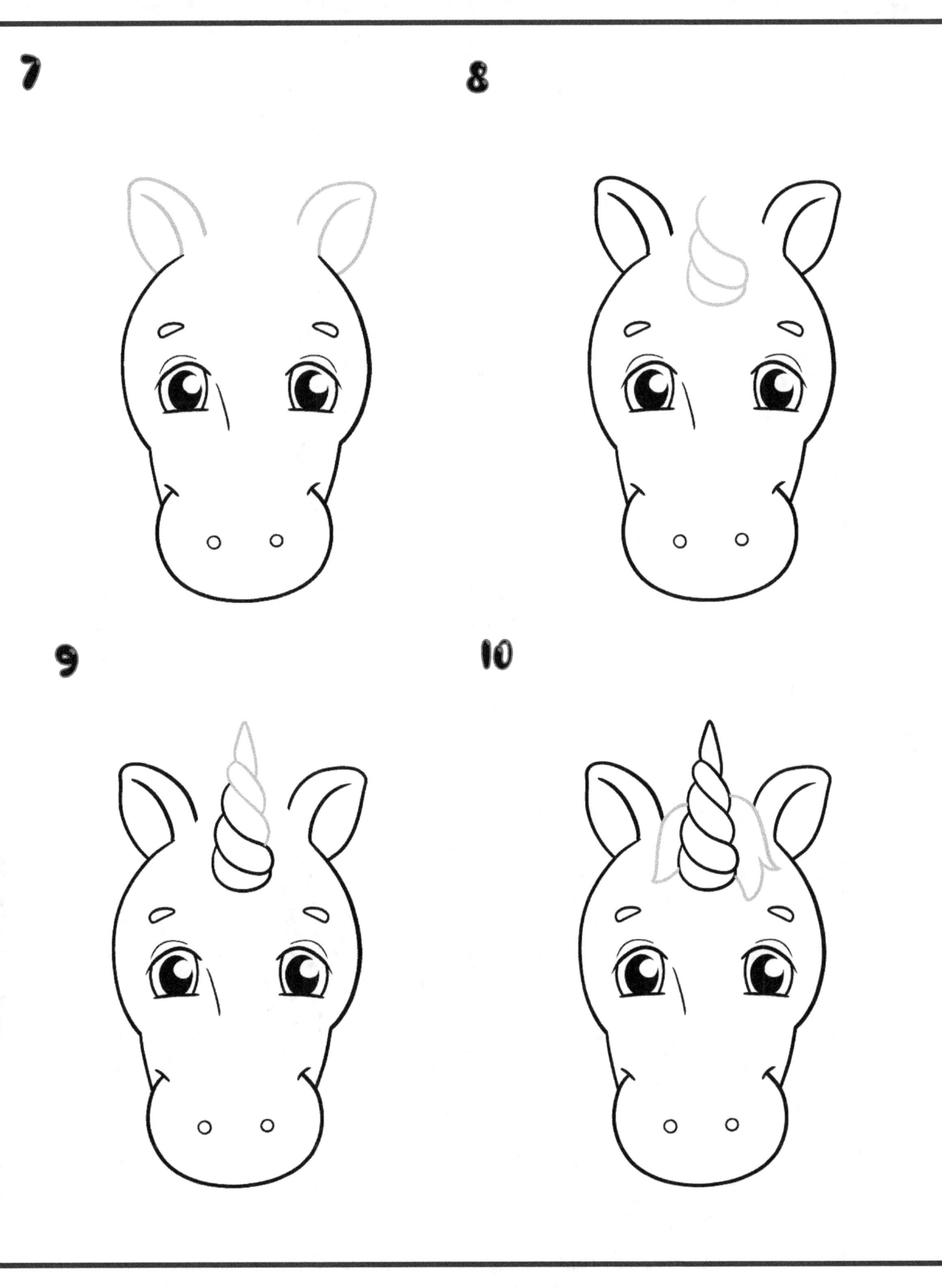

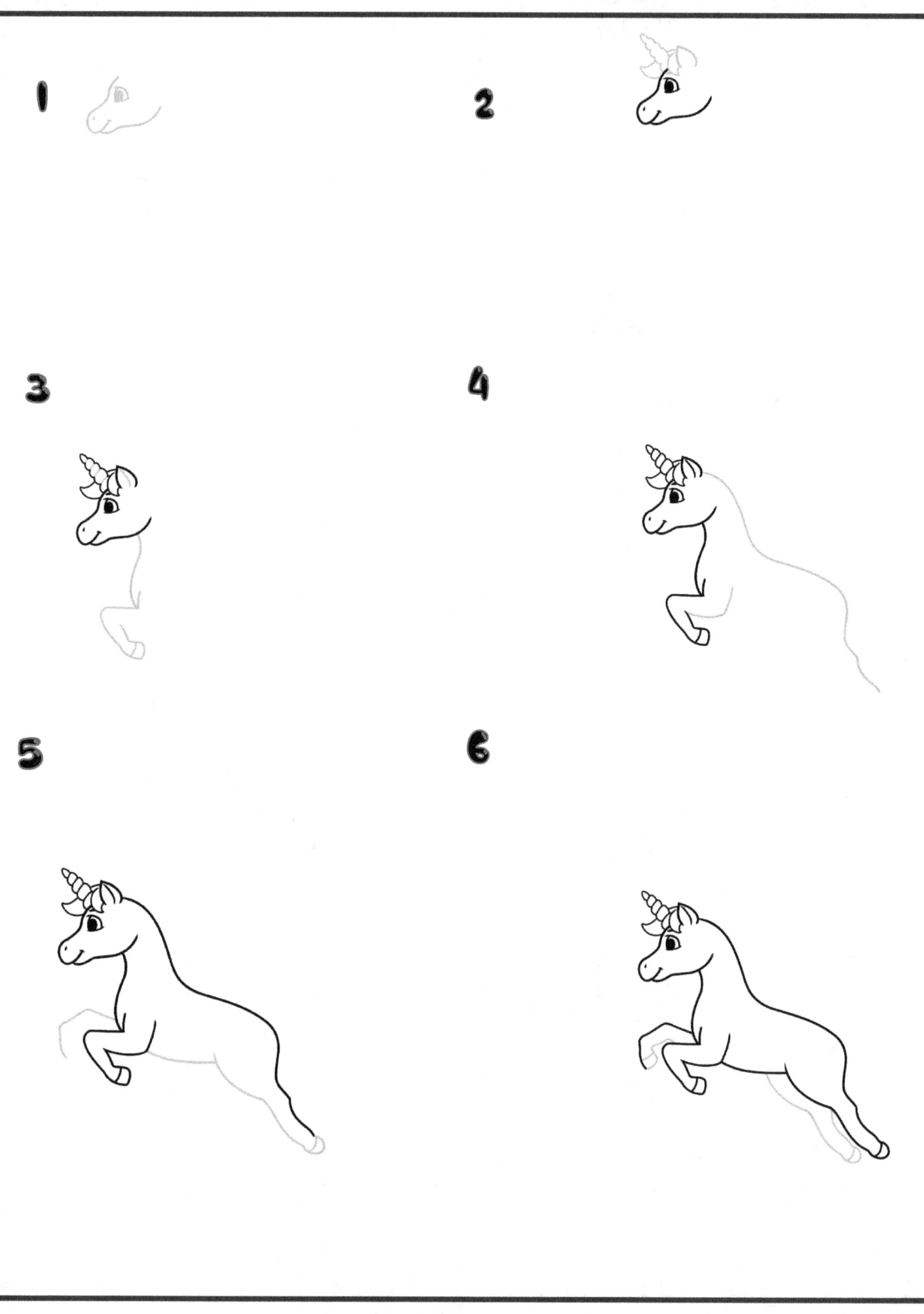

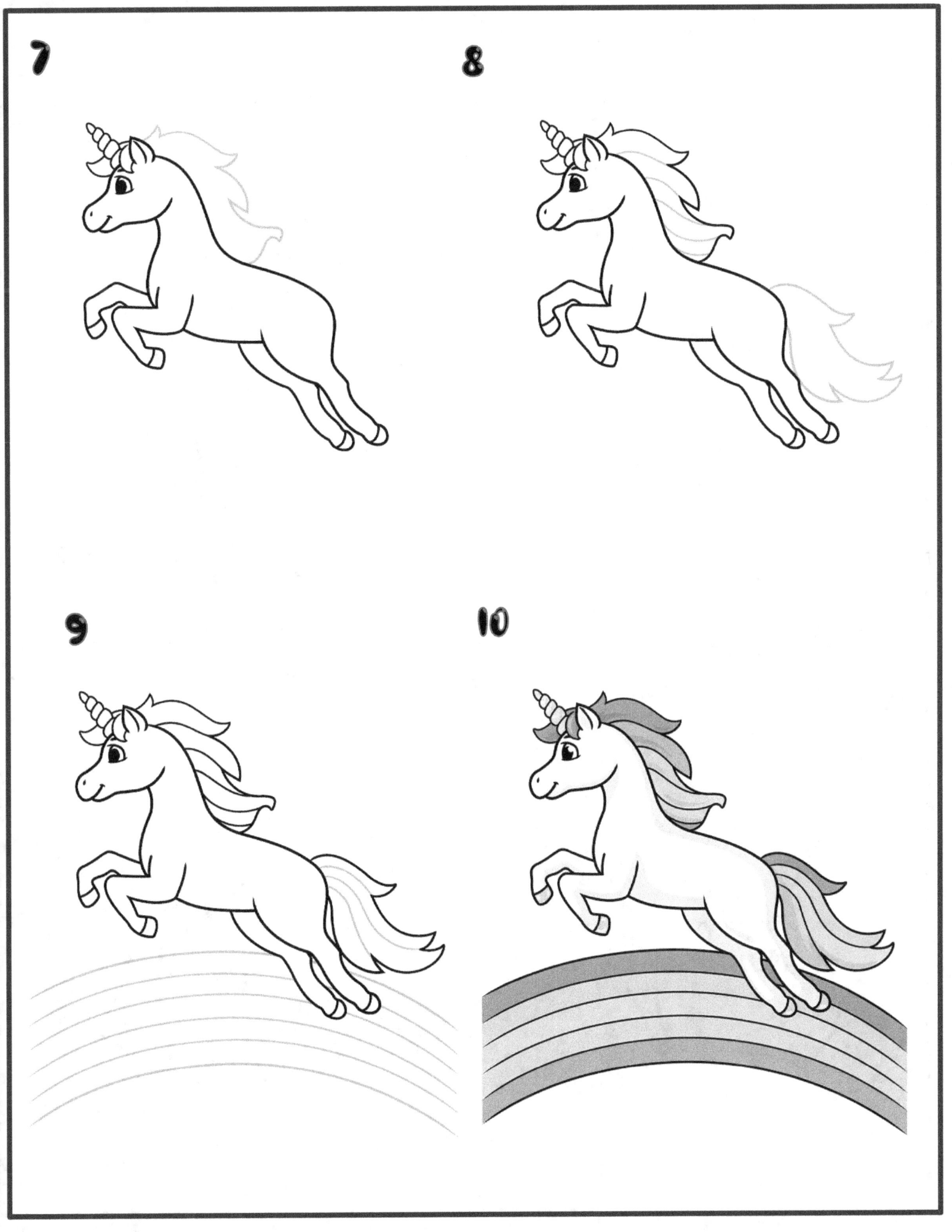

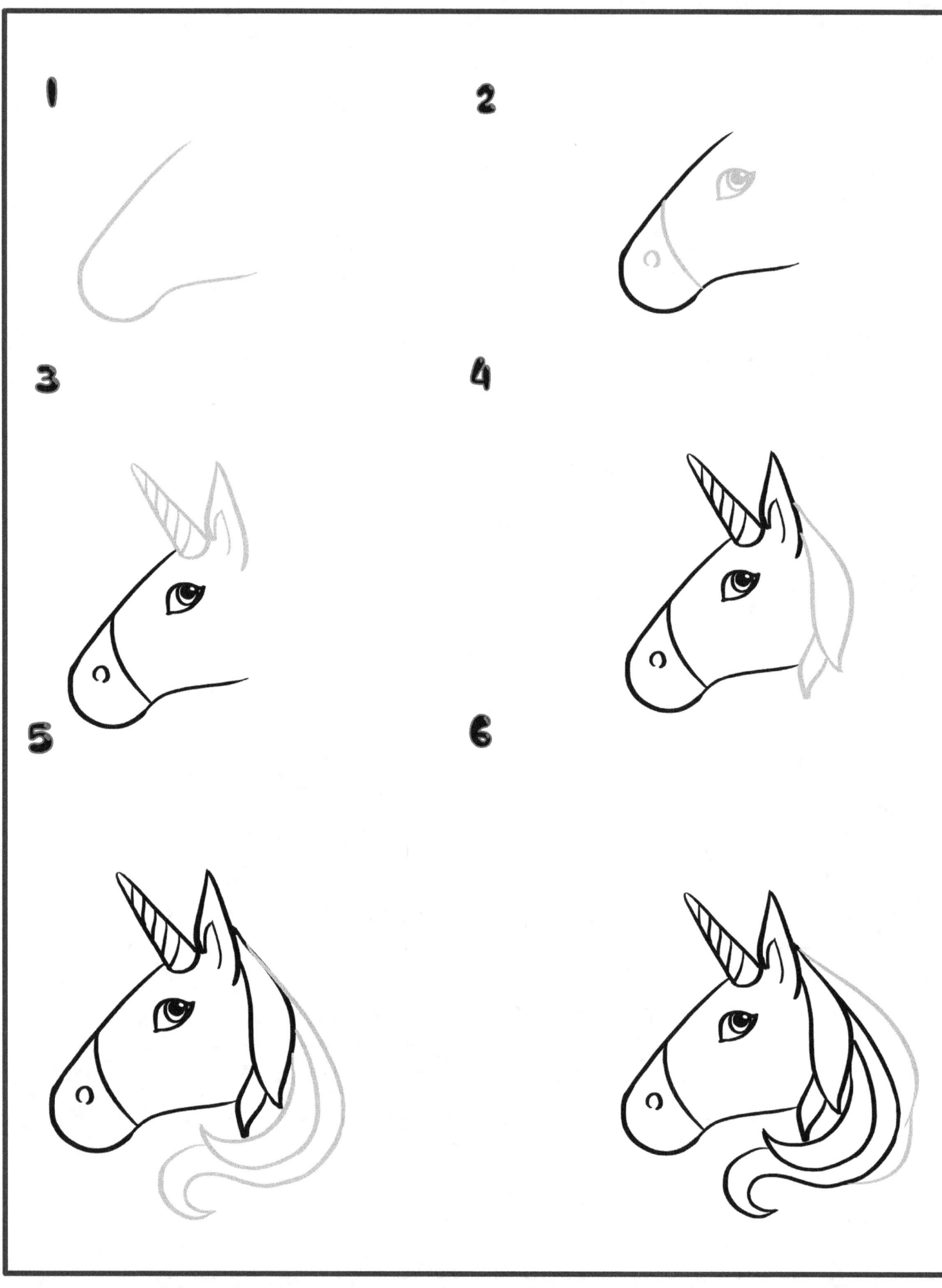

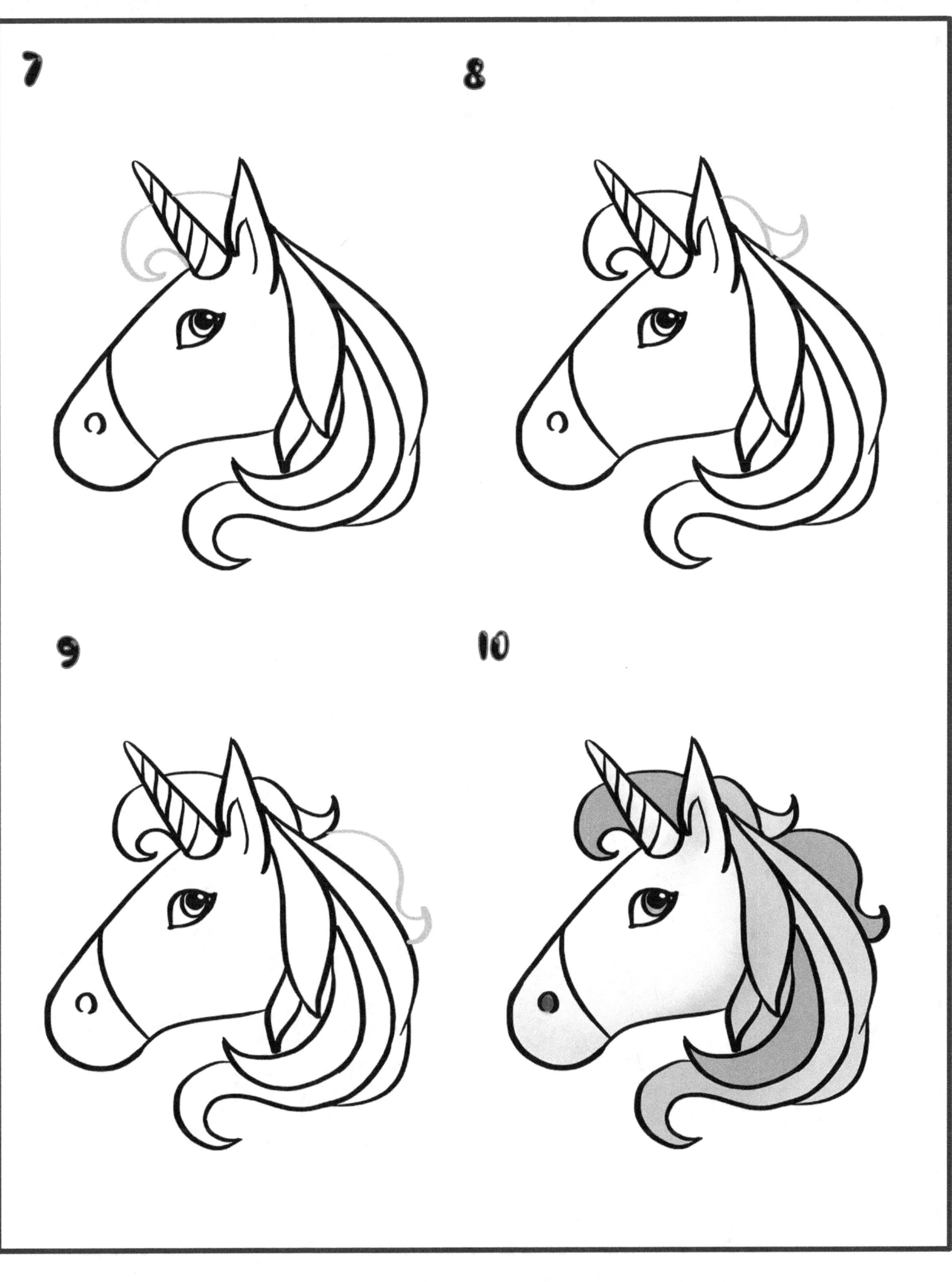

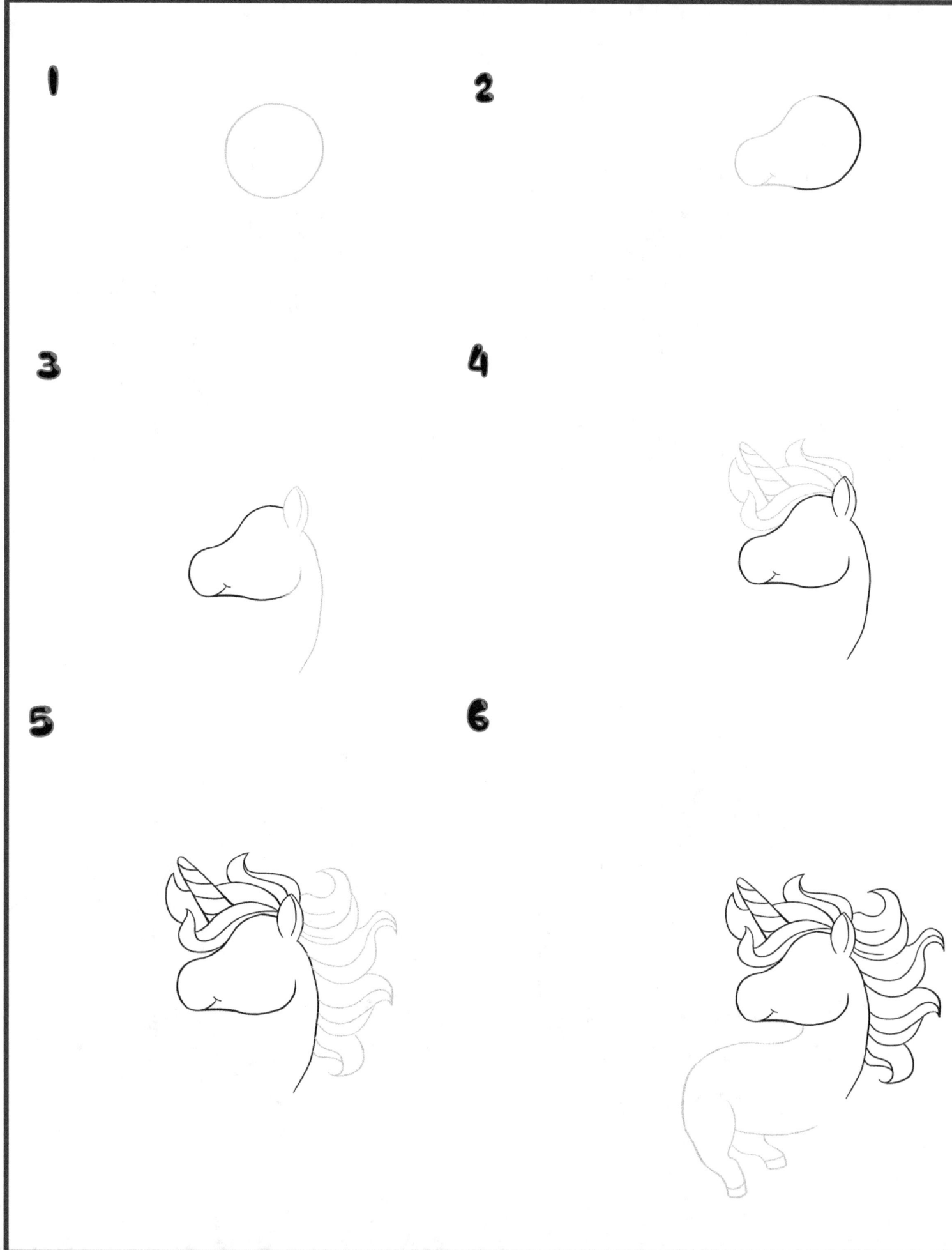

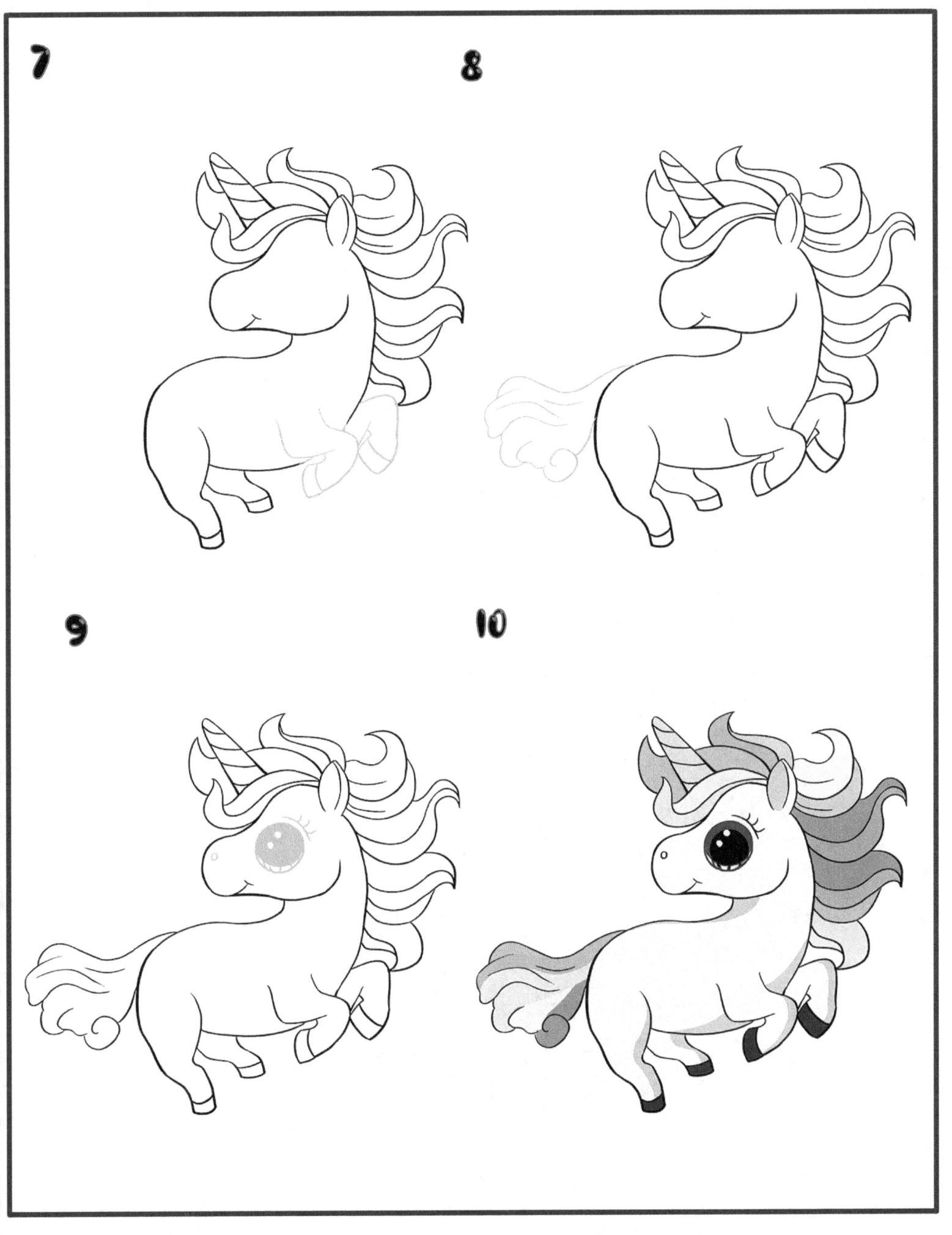

Part 3 how to draw a mermaid

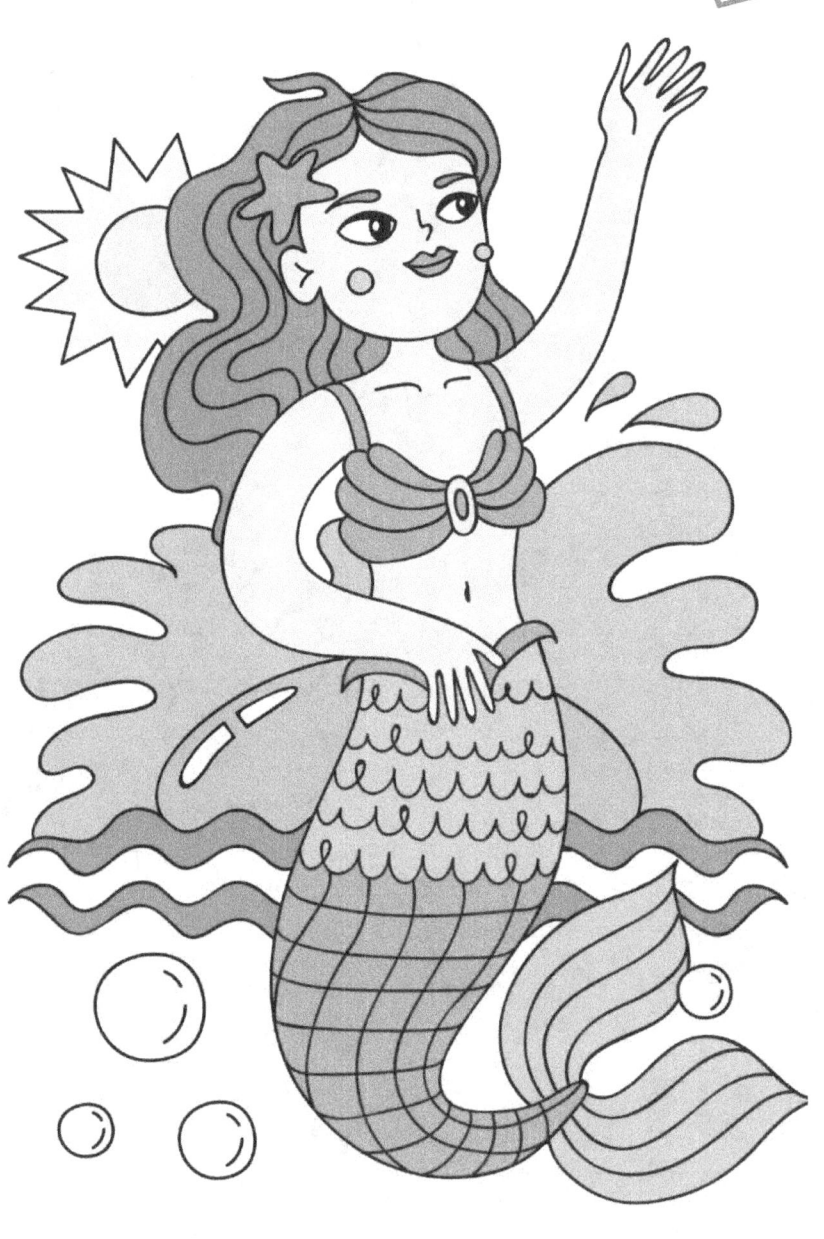

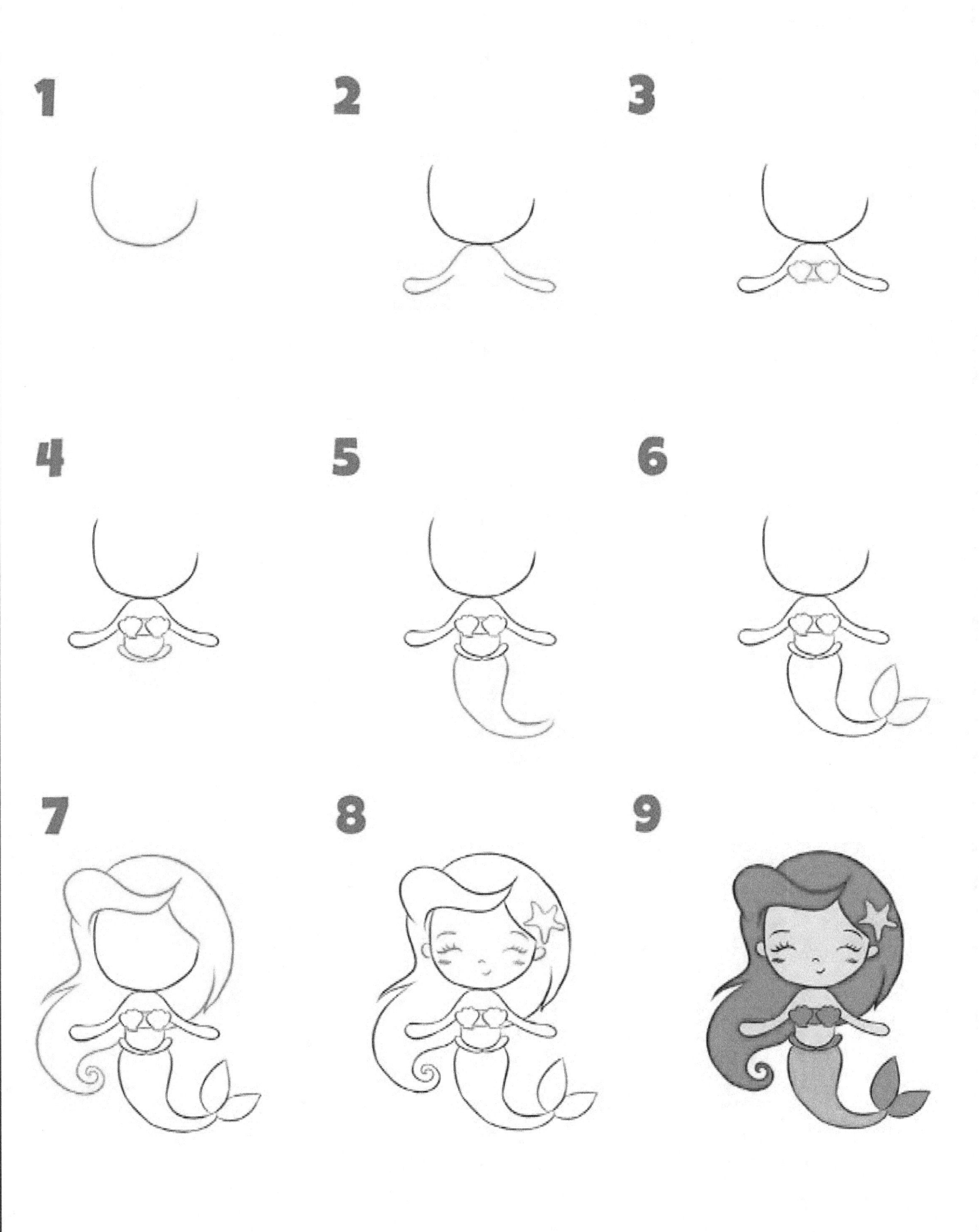

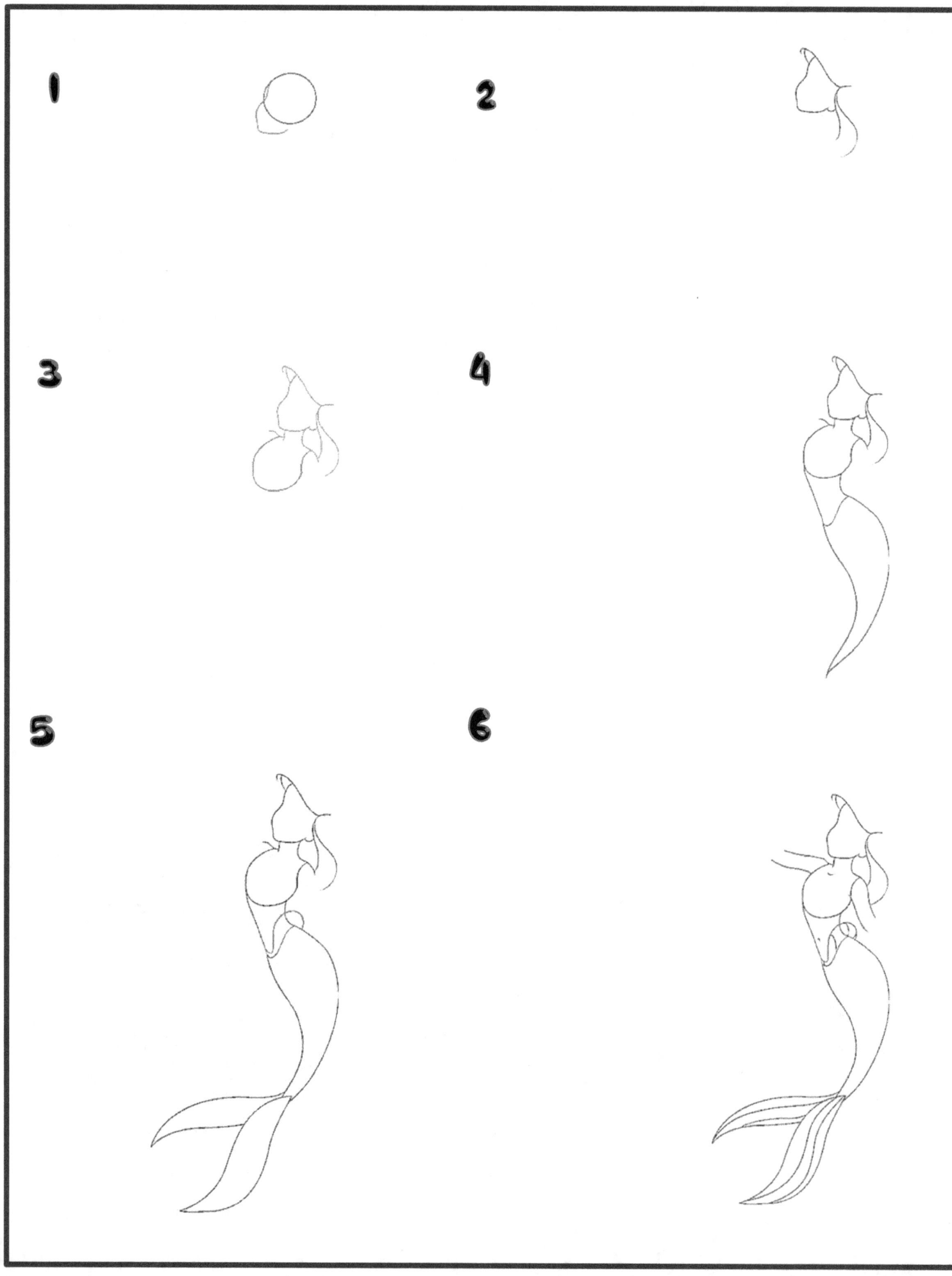

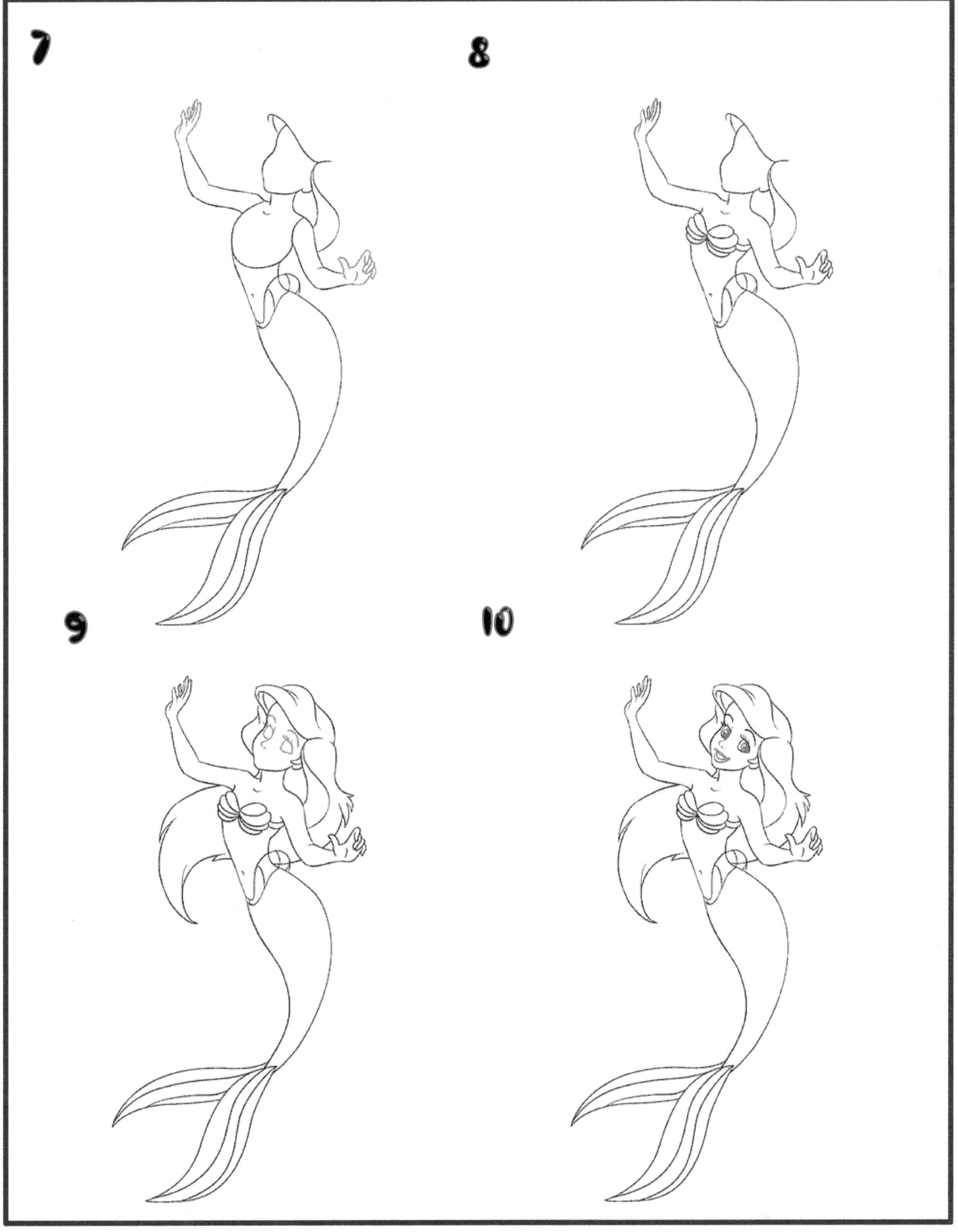

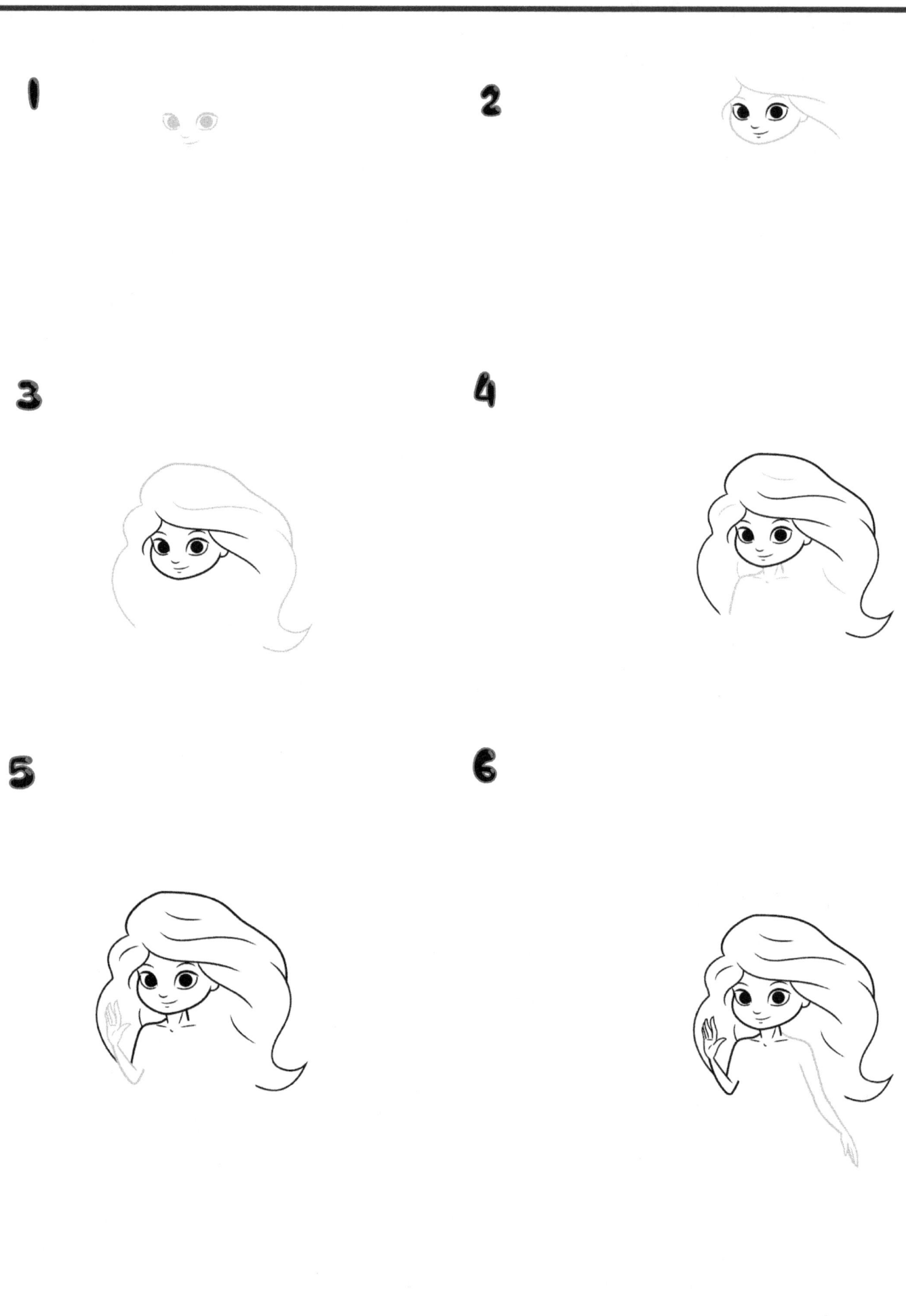

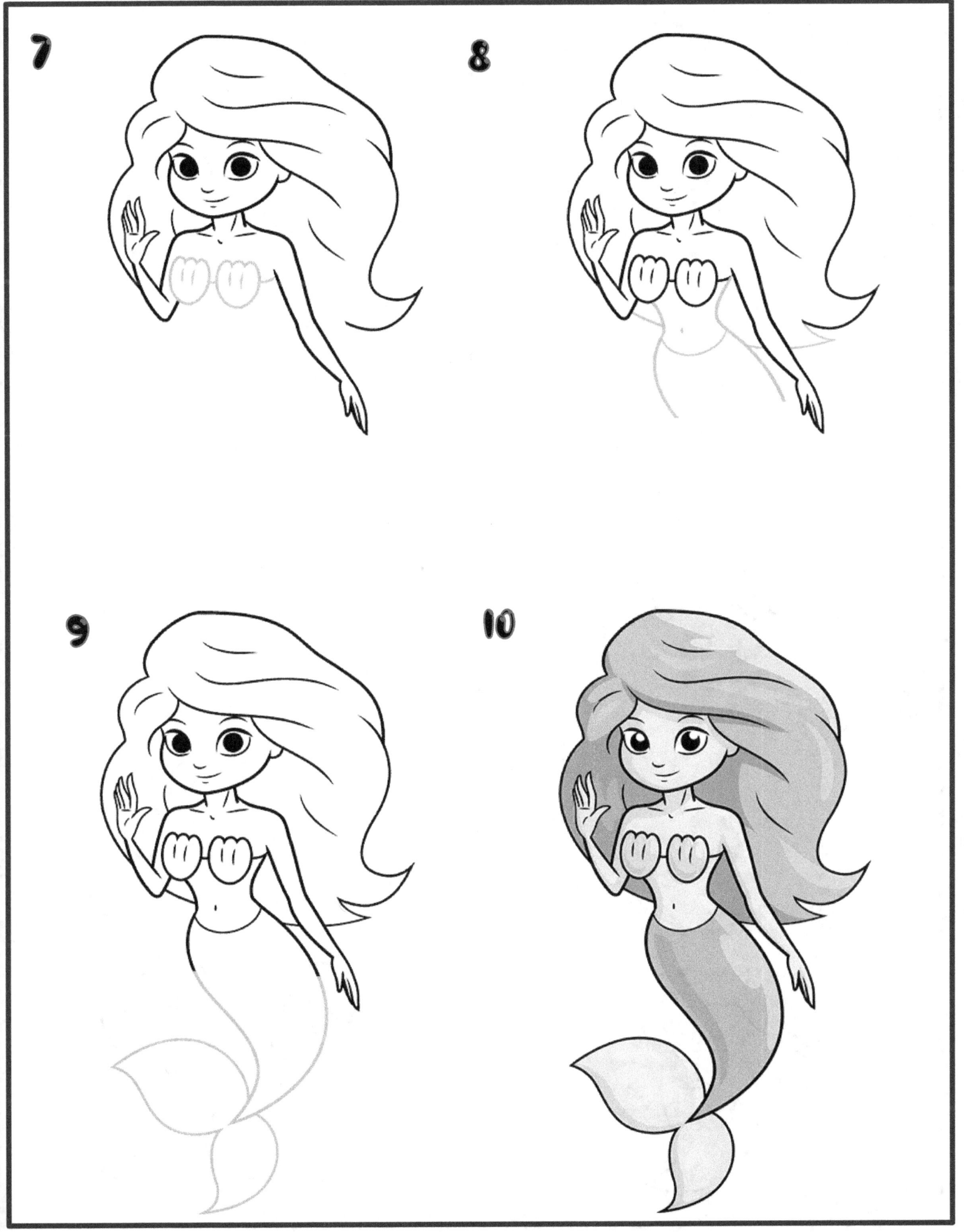

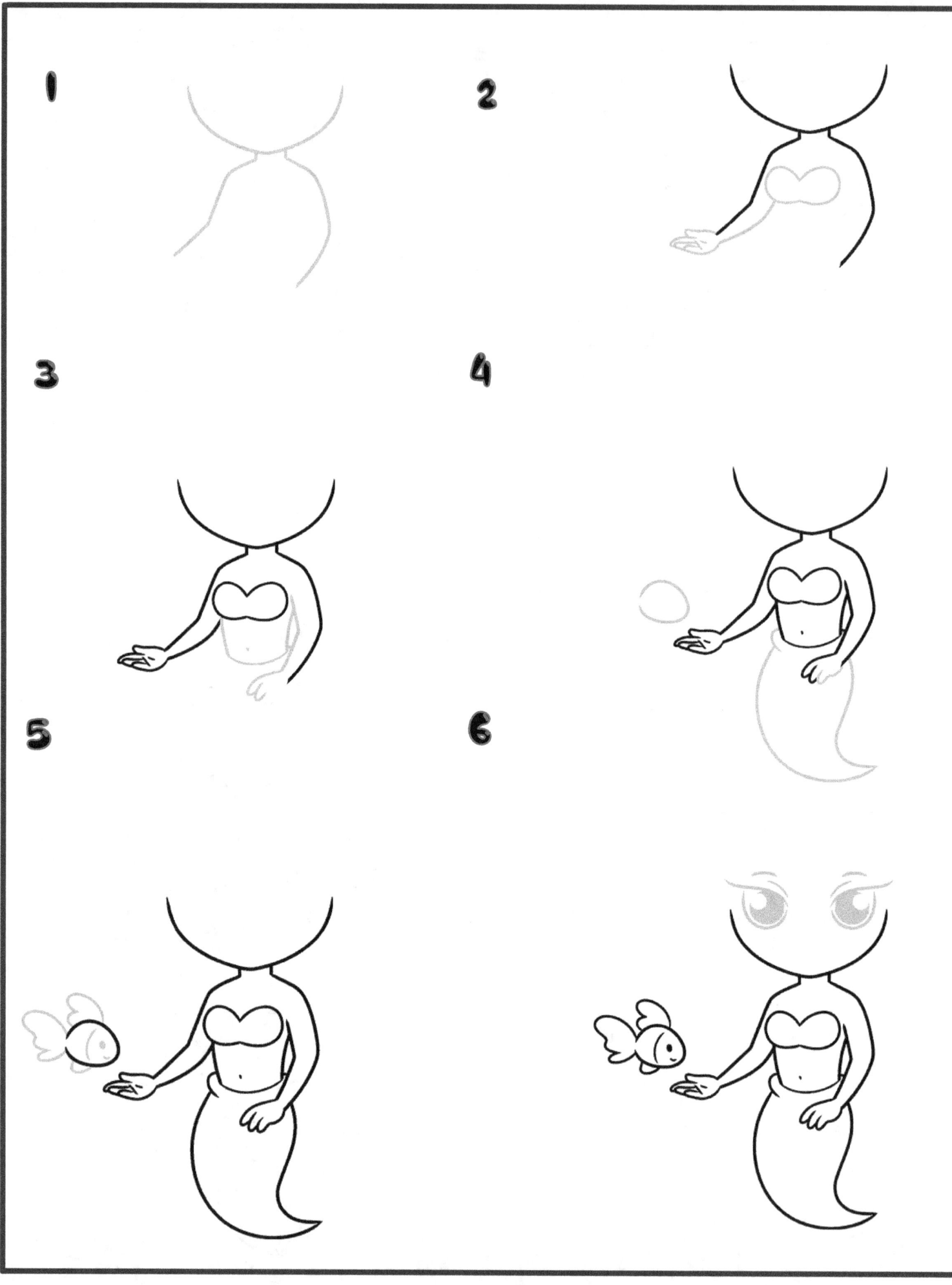

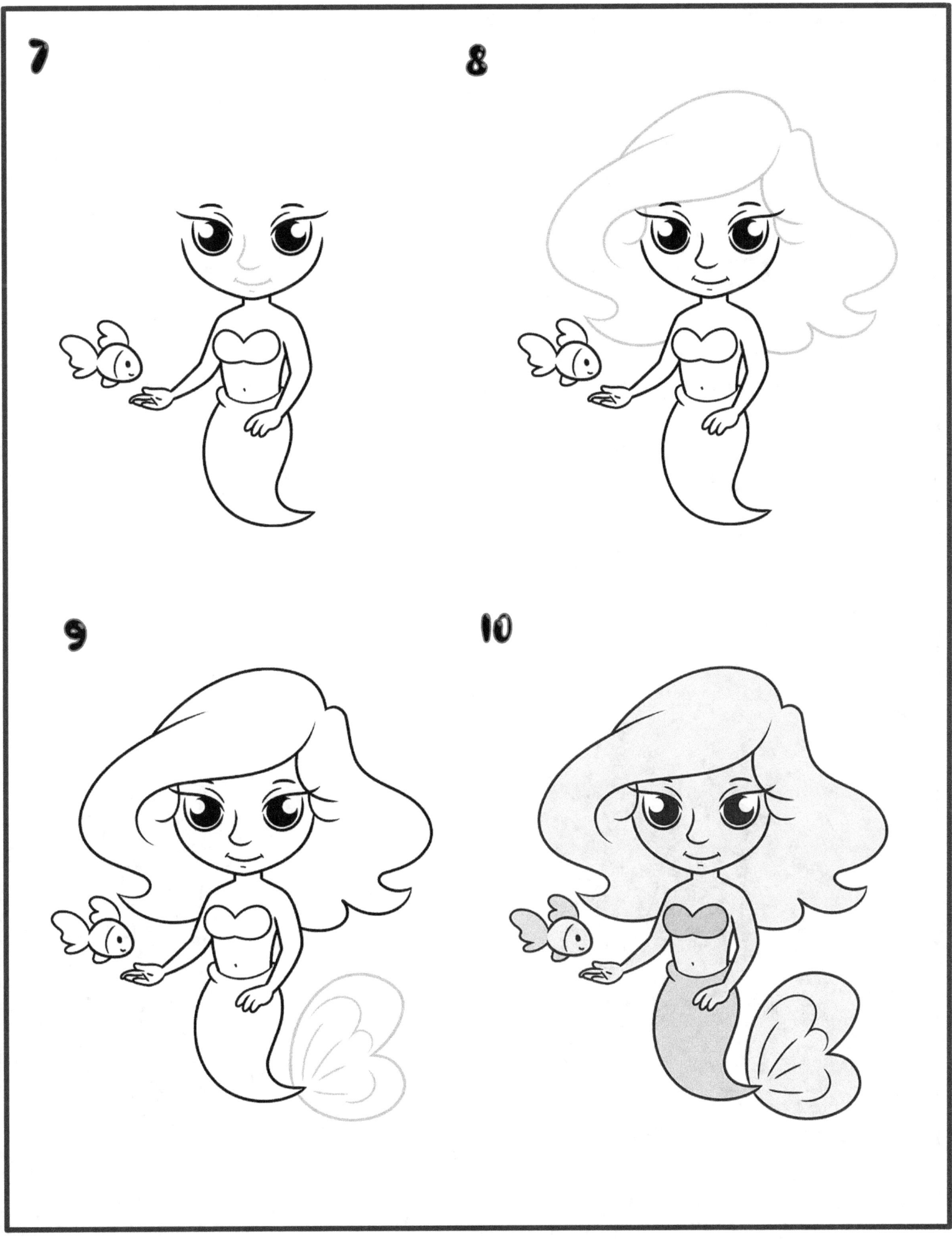

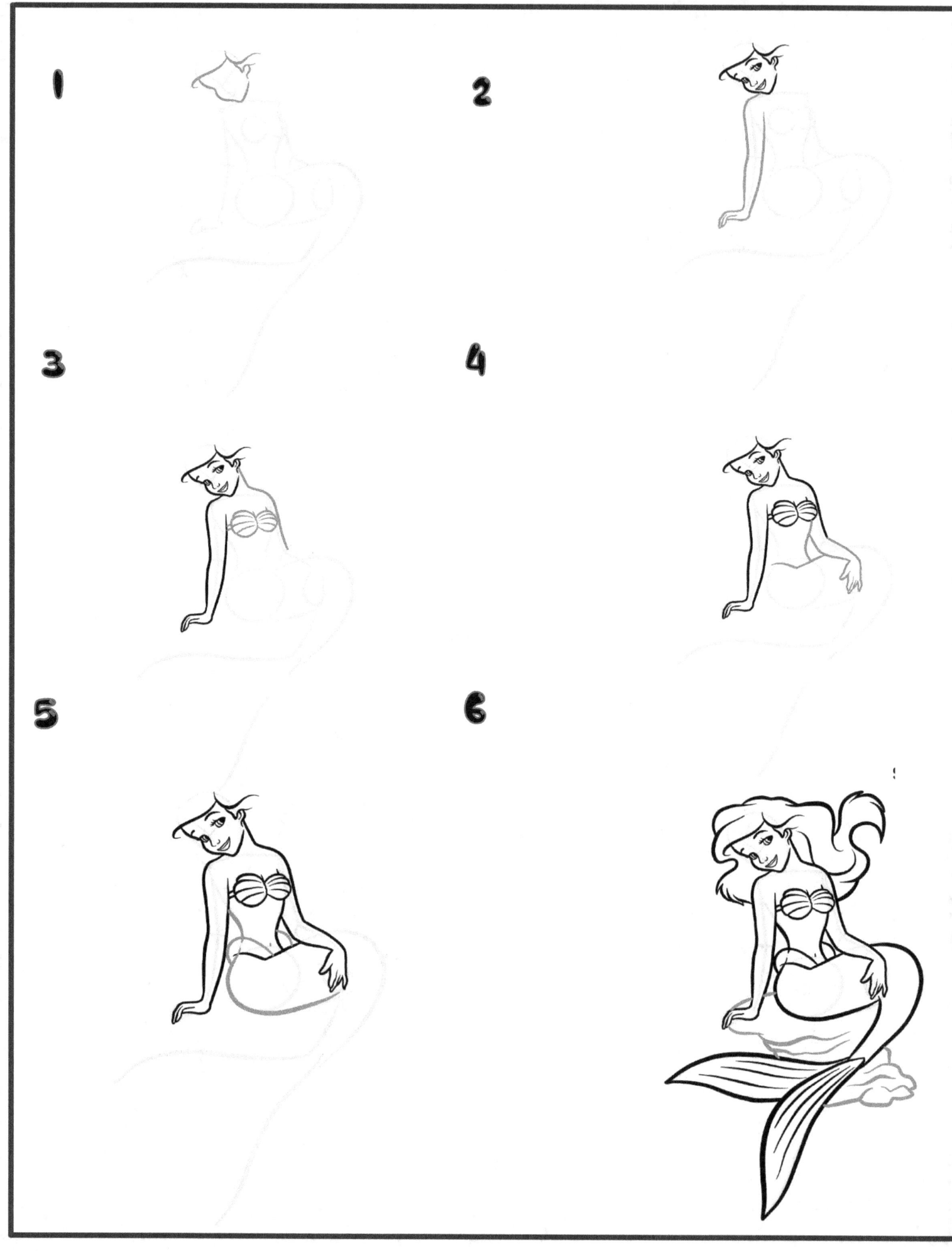

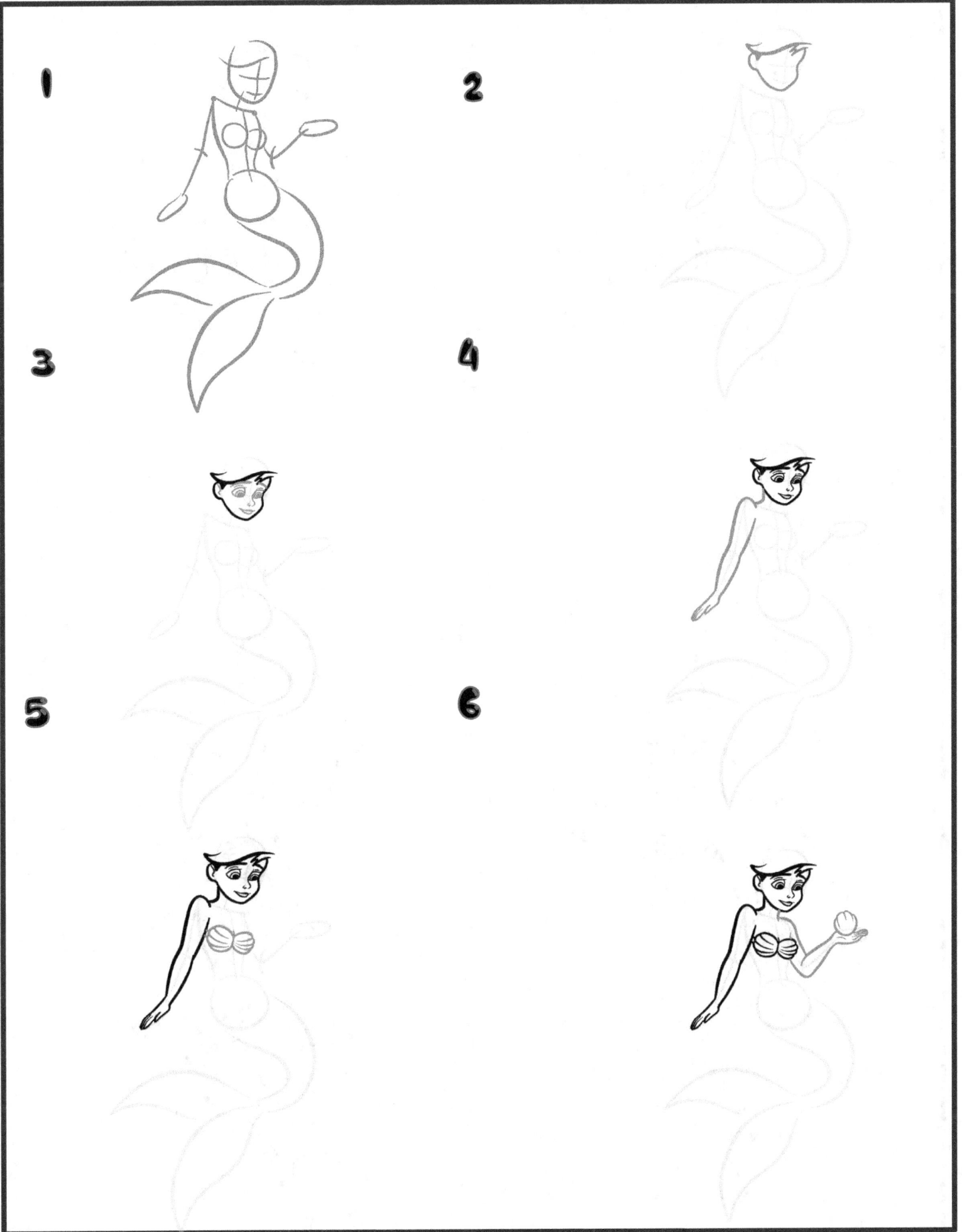

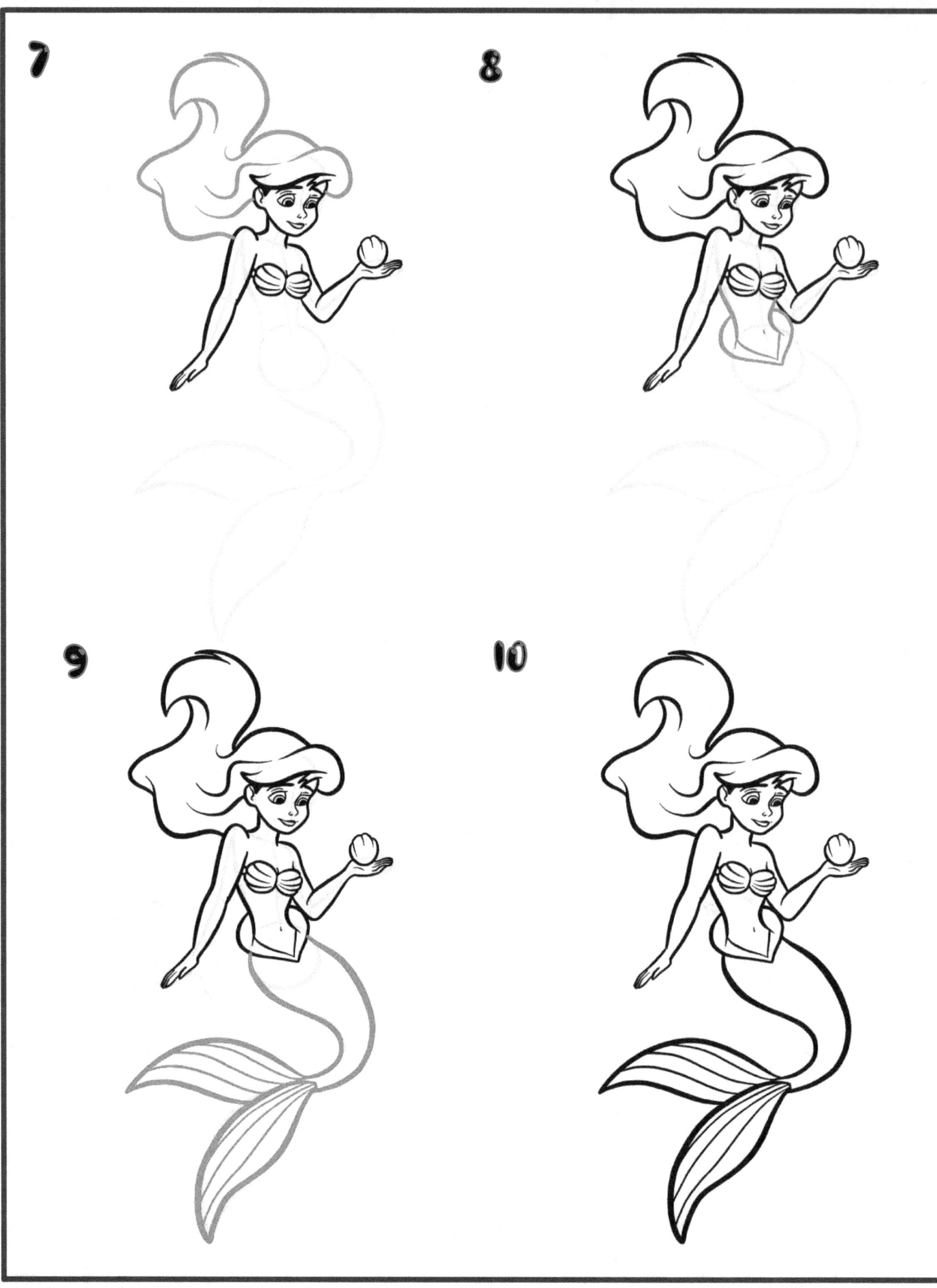

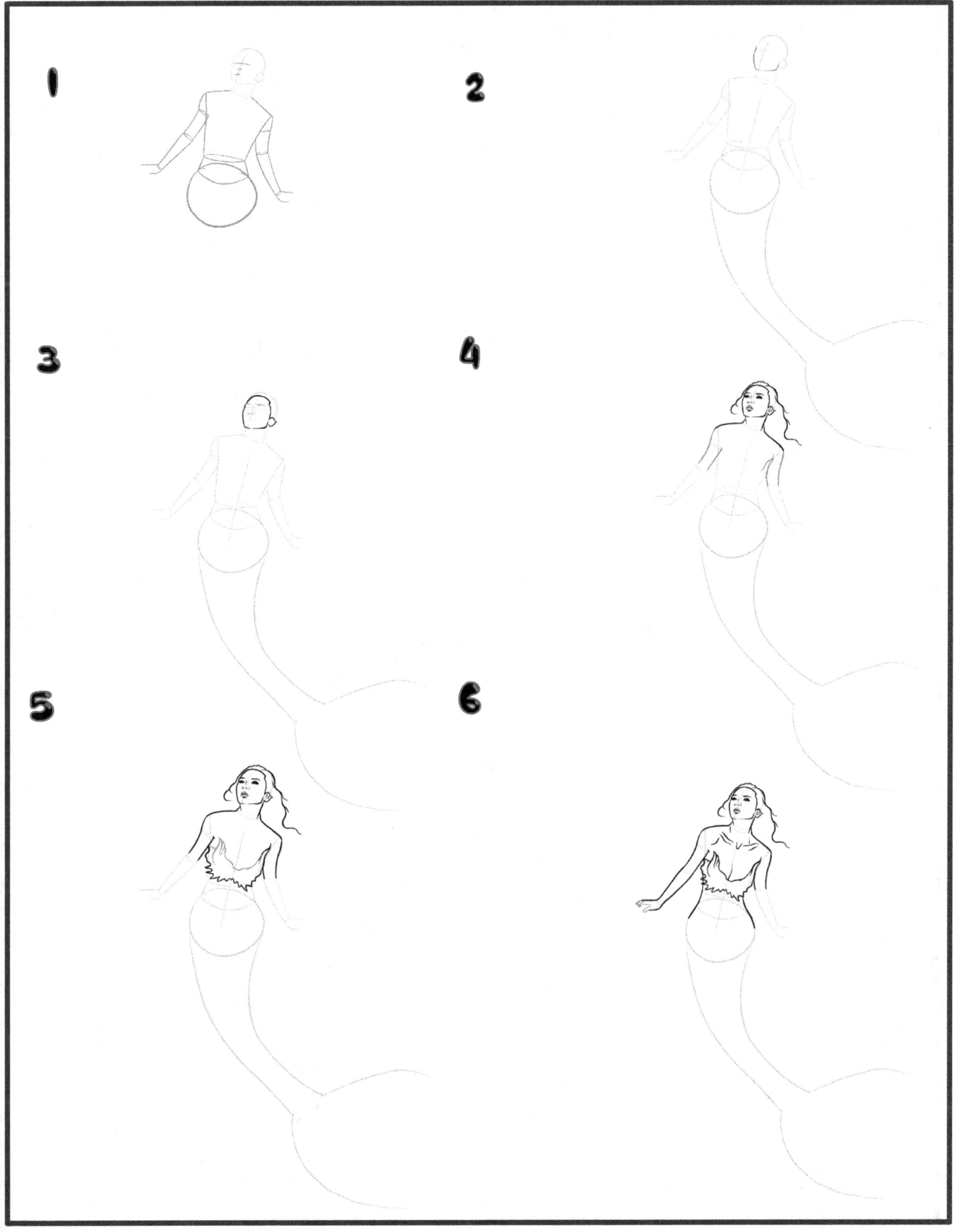

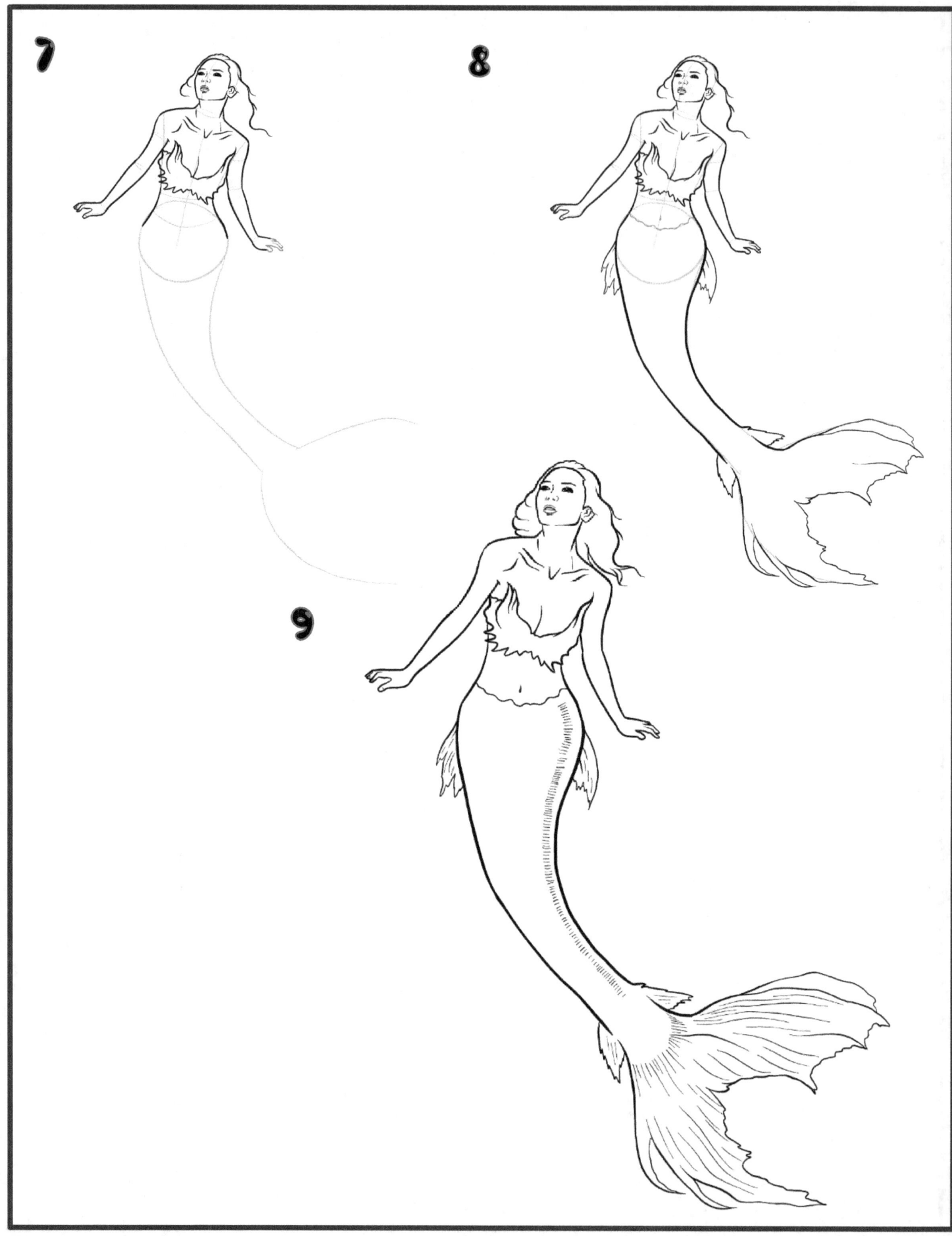

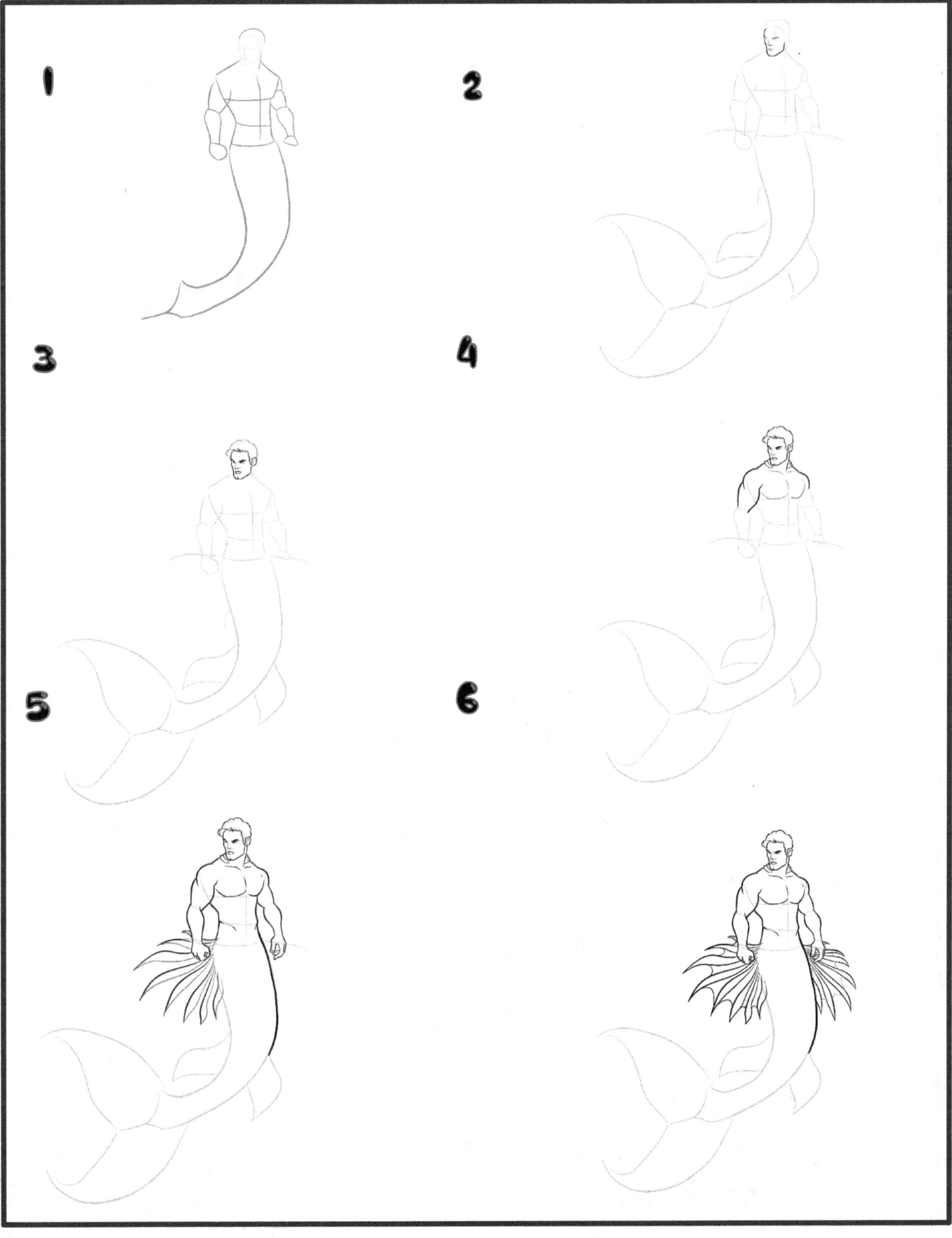

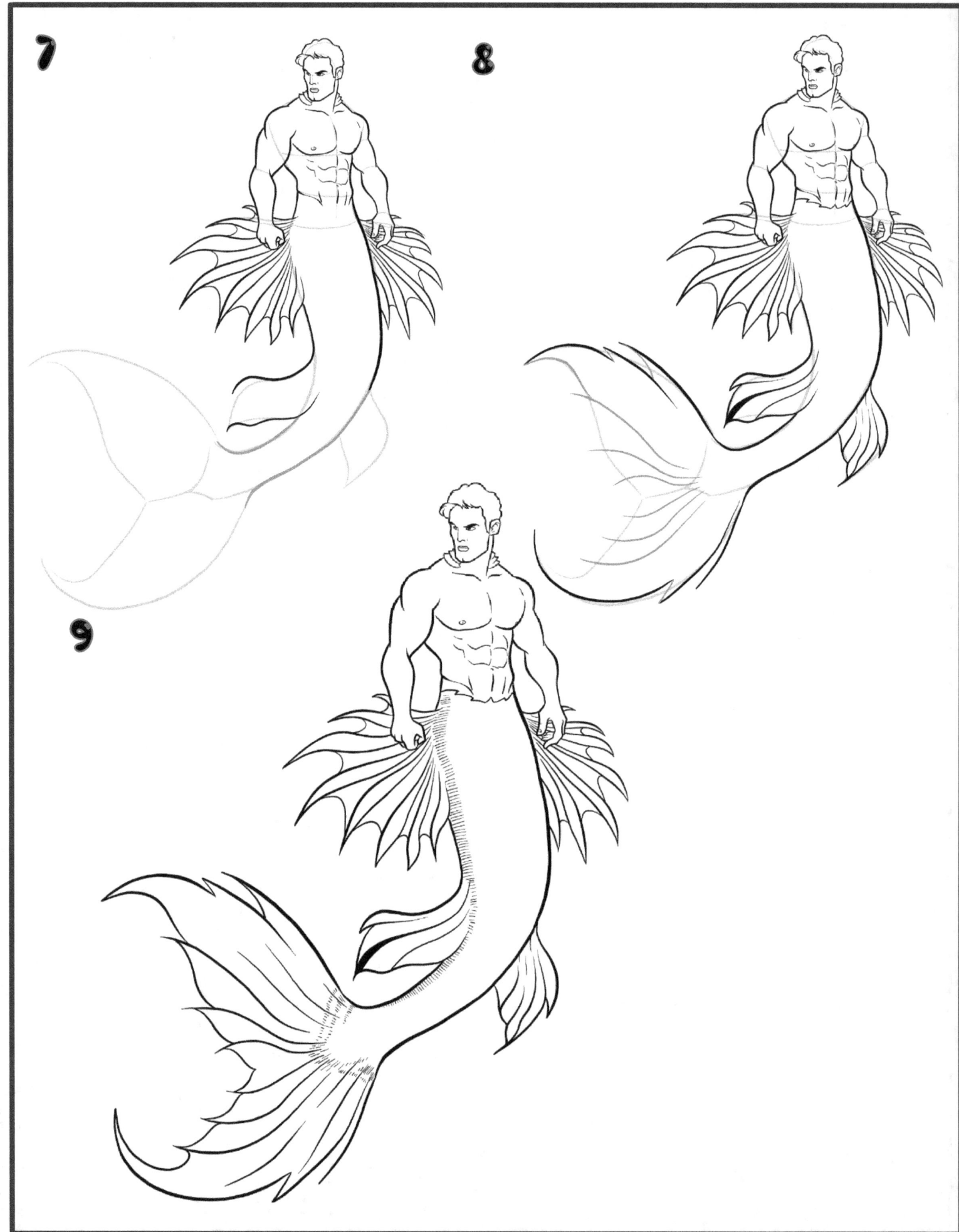

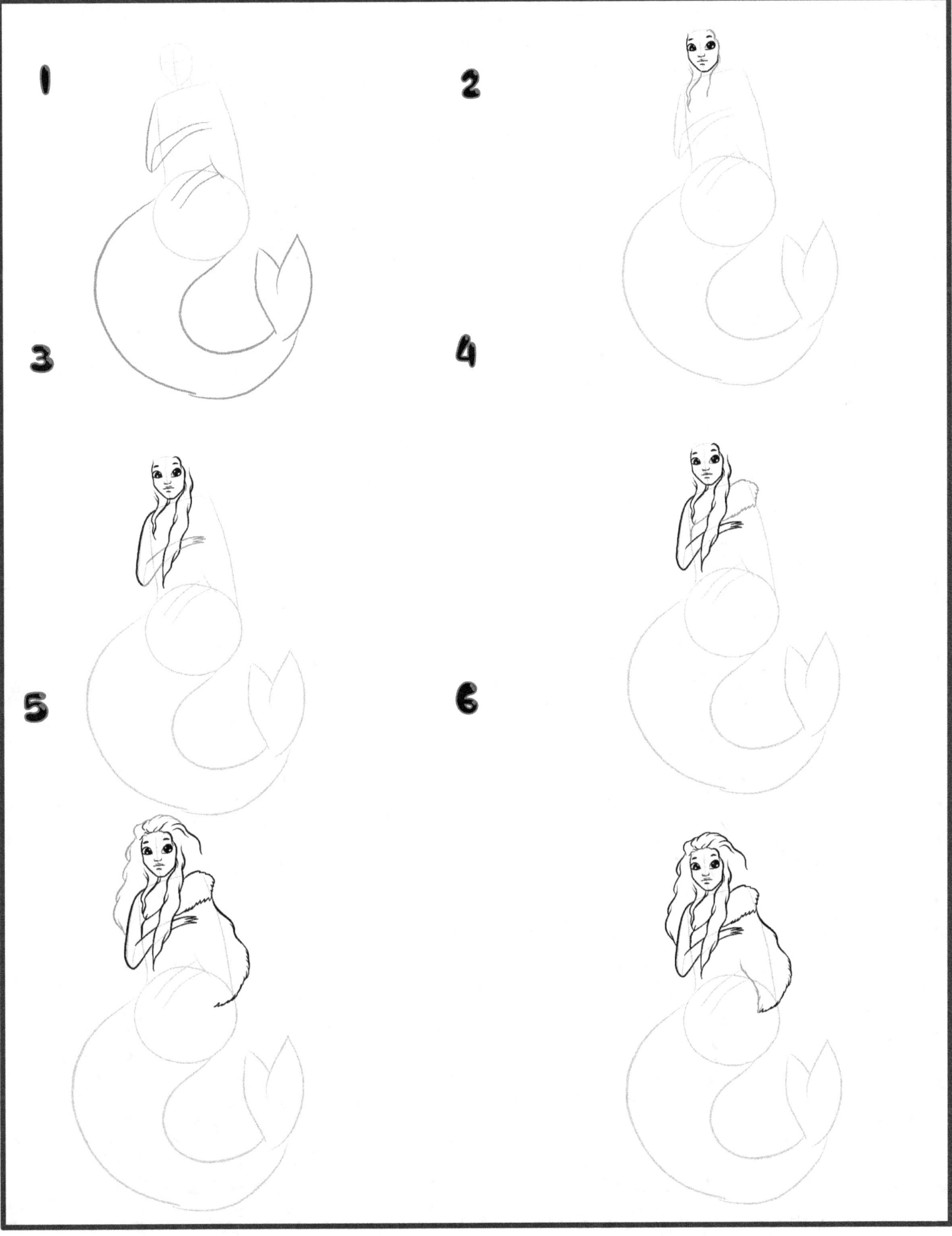

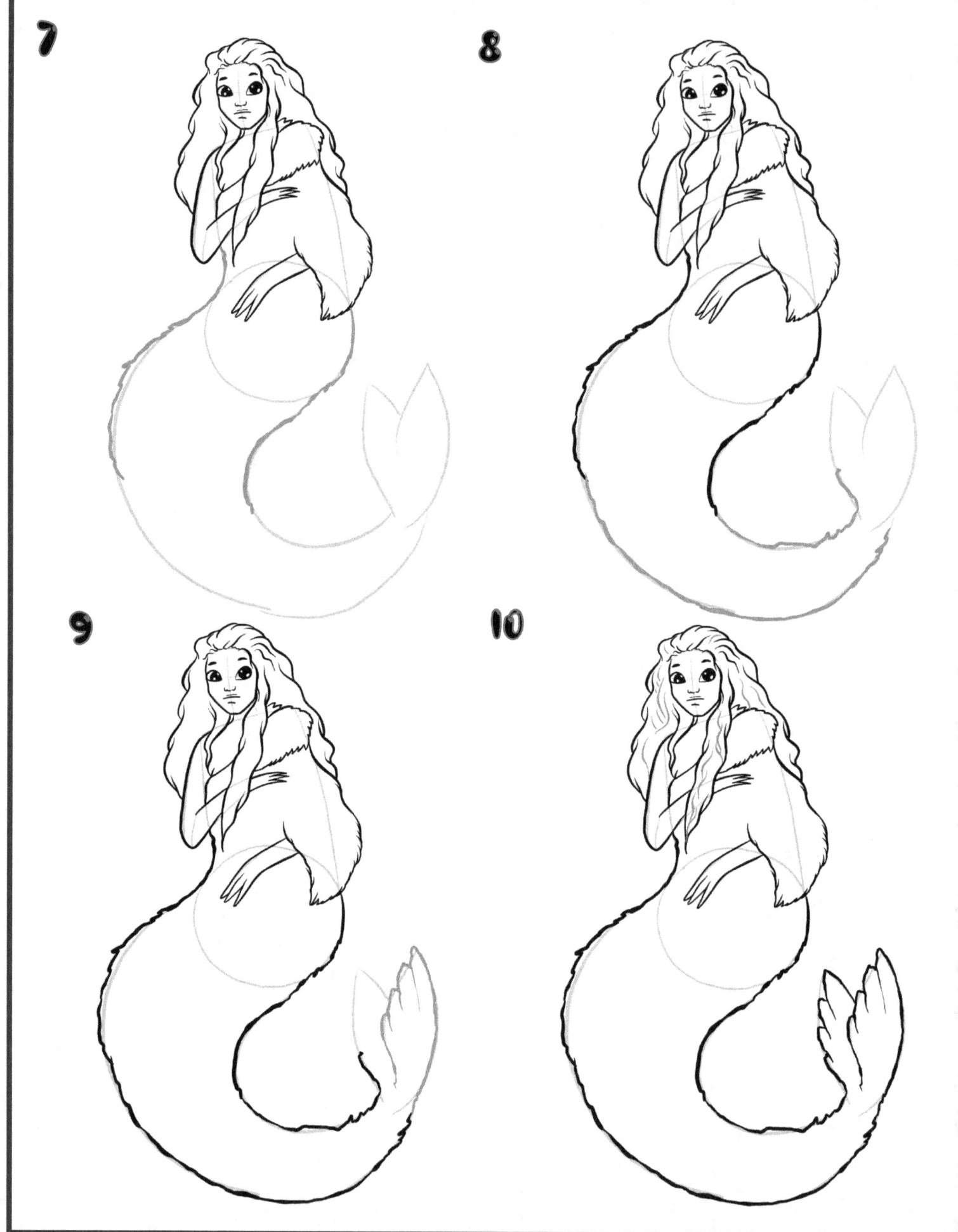

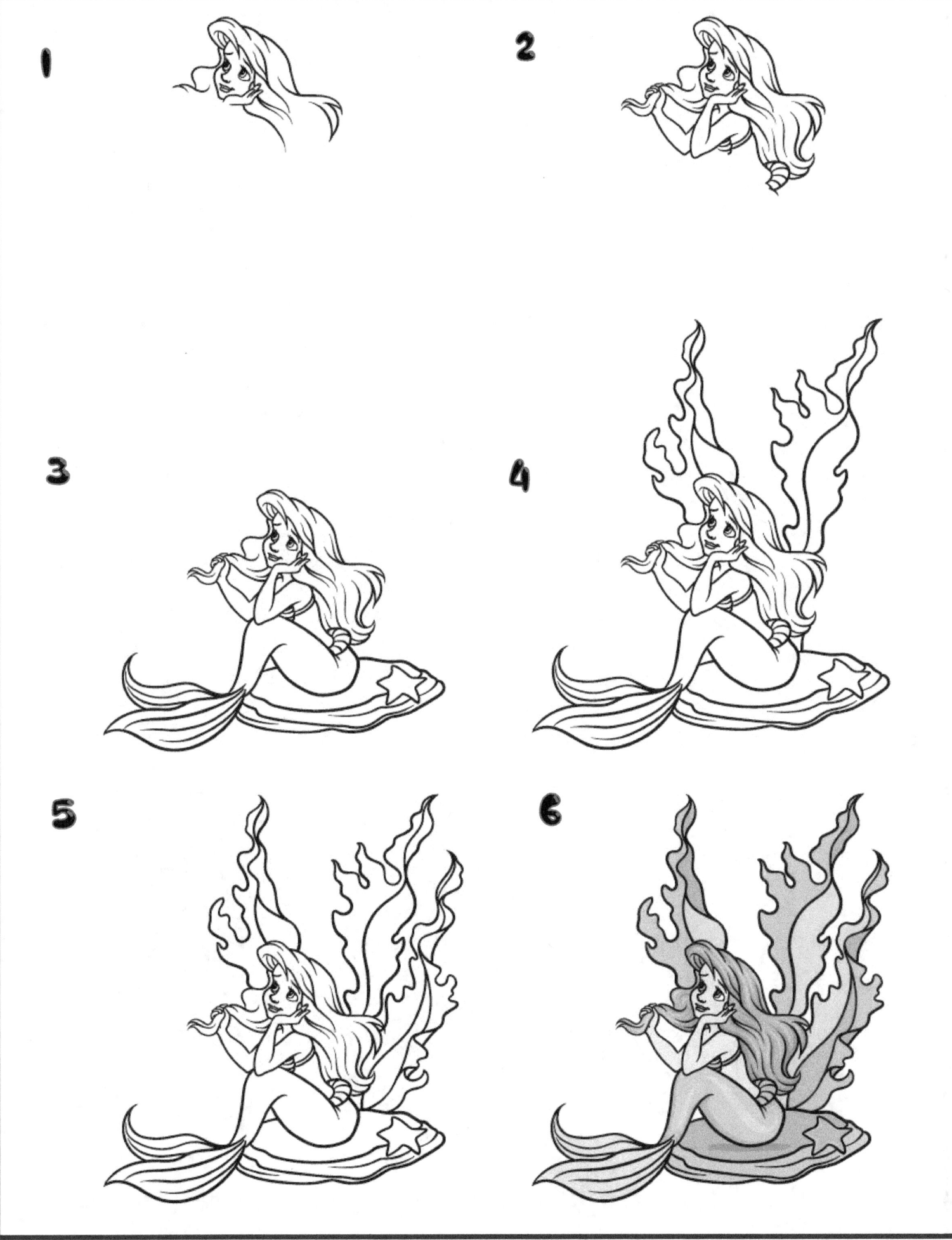

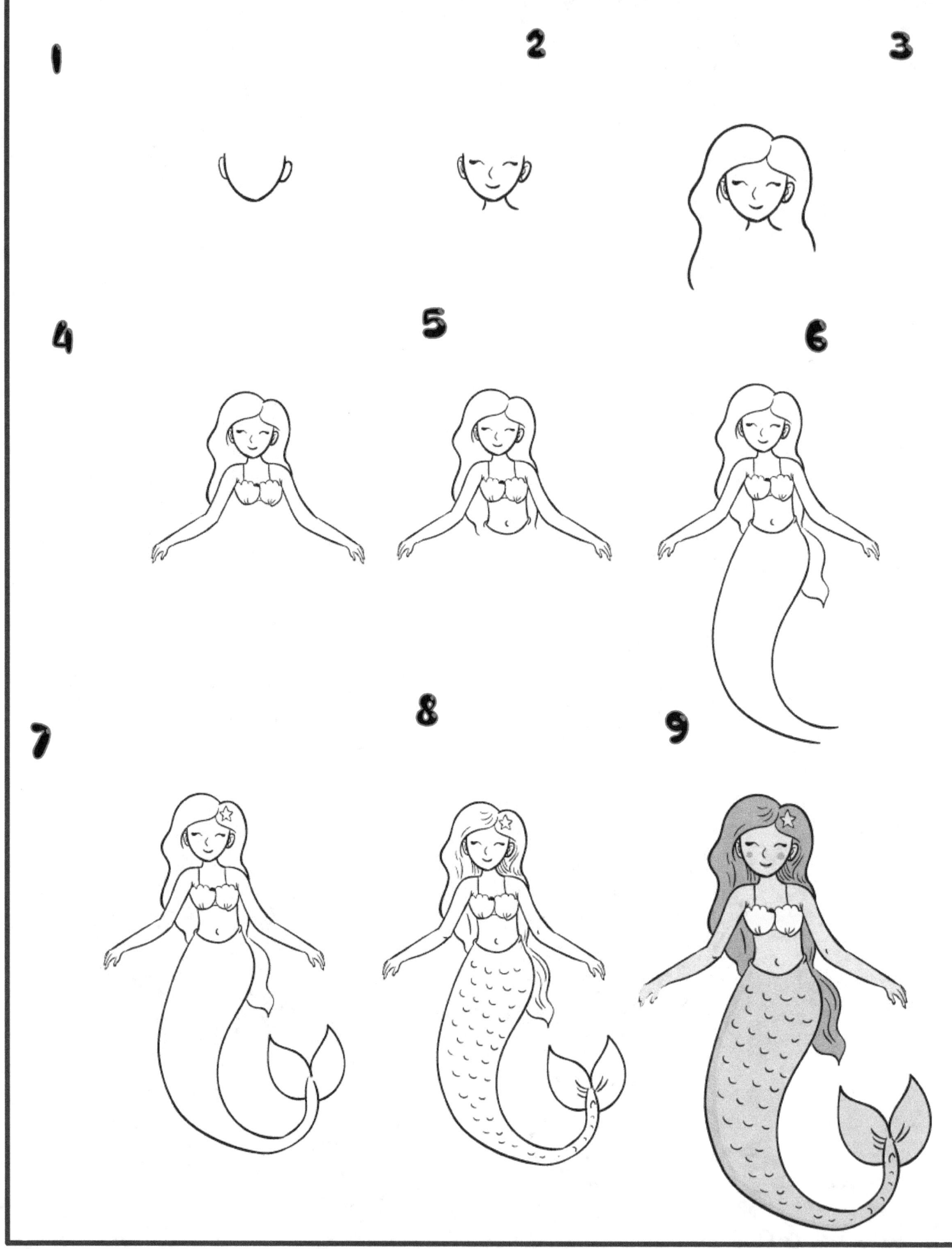

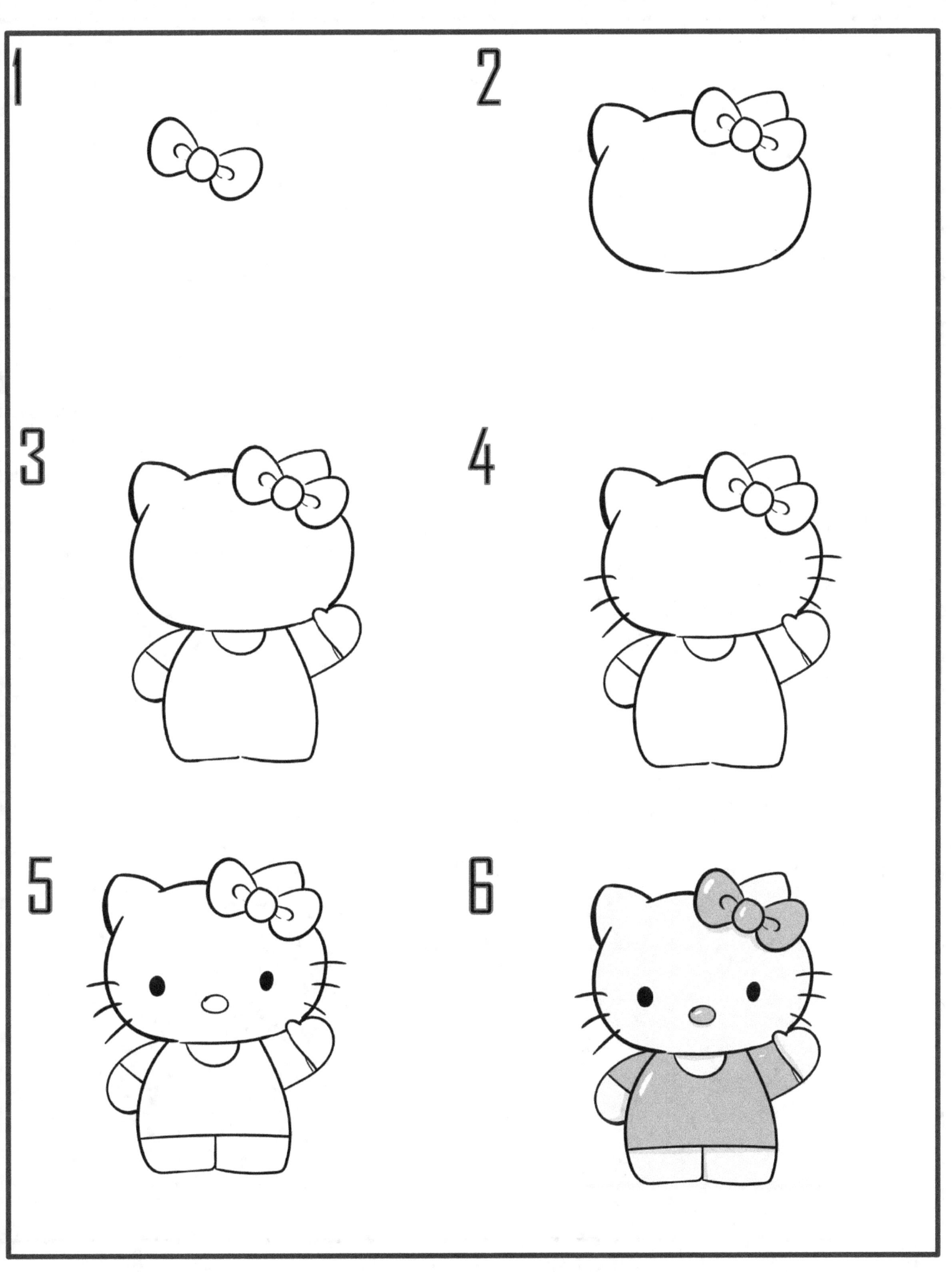

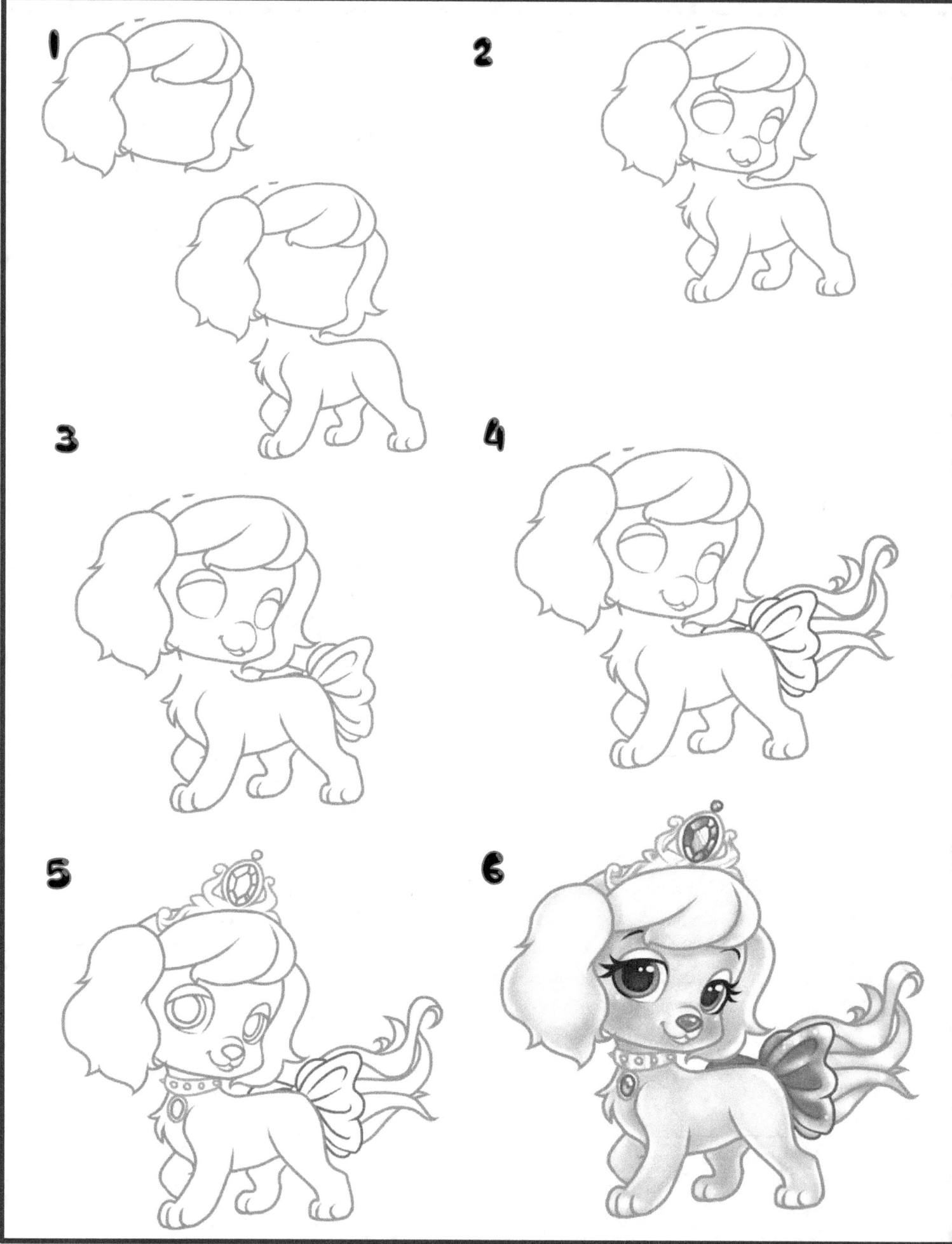

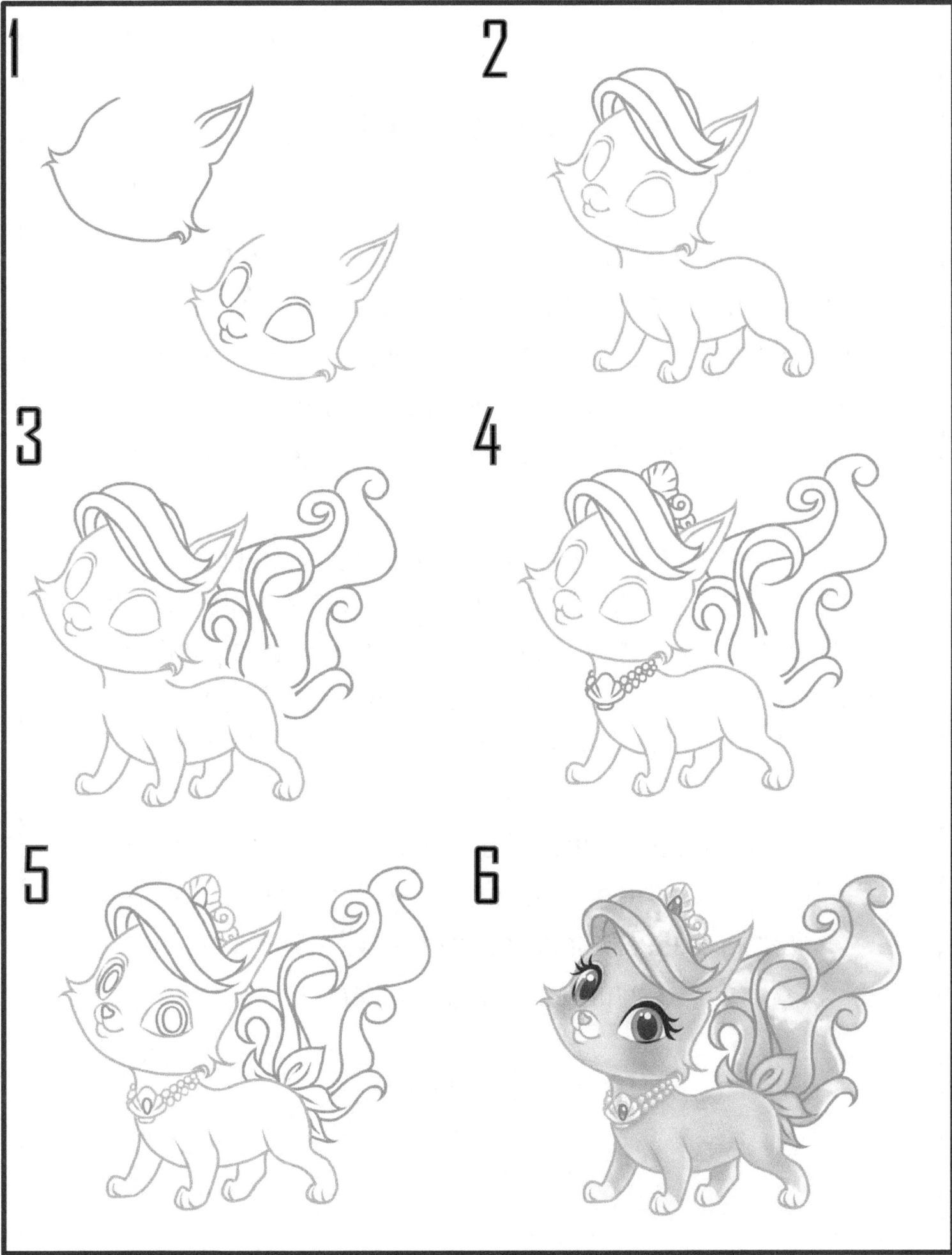

Nakhsa Katsuhito

Thank you for purchasing my book on Amazon. Your support and your interest in my work mean a lot to me. As an author and publisher, my goal is to create engaging and rewarding reading experiences. Your decision to invest in my book validates my efforts and I am truly grateful.

I am asking for your help in publishing my book. Your comments are invaluable not only to me but to other readers as well. If you liked the book, be sure to leave a positive review on Amazon. Your opinion can have a significant impact and help potential readers discover the world I create.

Thank you for being part of my writing journey. Your enthusiasm and dedication inspire me to continue writing stories that resonate with readers like you. I really appreciate your support.

warmest regards,